Earth Ponds A to Z

Earth Ponds A to Z

AN ILLUSTRATED ENCYCLOPEDIA

Tim Matson

Illustrated by Frank Fretz

The Countryman Press
Woodstock, Vermont

First Edition

Library of Congress Cataloging-in-Publication Data
Matson, Tim
Earth Ponds A to Z : an illustrated encyclopedia / Tim Matson.—1st ed.
p. cm.
Includes bibliographical references.
ISBN 0-88150-494-7
1. Water-supply, Rural—Encyclopedias. 2. Ponds—Encyclopedias. I. Title.
TD927.M43397 2003
627'.14—dc21

2002067672

Cover and interior design by Carrie Fradkin
Cover and interior illustrations © Frank Fretz

Published by The Countryman Press, P.O. Box 748, Woodstock, Vermont 05091
Distributed by W.W. Norton & Company, 500 Fifth Avenue, New York, NY 10110
Printed in the United States of America
10 9 8 7 6 5 4 3 2

Dedication

This book is dedicated to the pond builders.

Contents

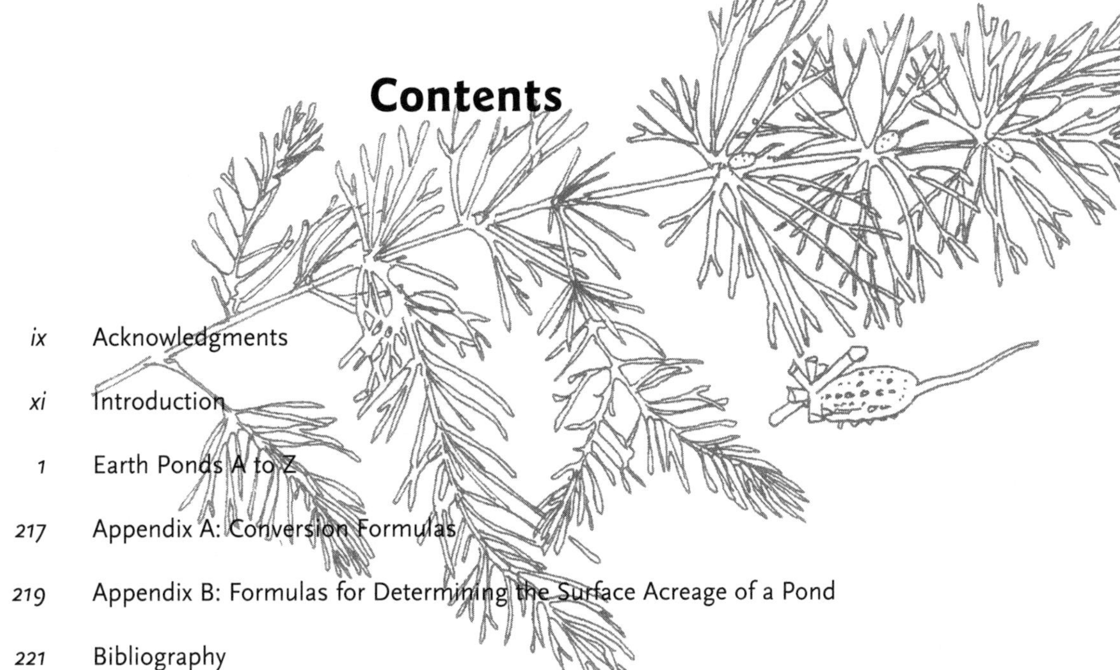

Acknowledgments

Thanks are due to all those who generously shared knowledge, lore, stories, and hunches. In particular, I wish to acknowledge the contribution of several pond builders who were always ready to help answer questions, offer suggestions, and remind me that sometimes there are no sure solutions, so take your best shot: Noel Dydo, Ted Kenyon, Brian Kenyon, and Gary Ulman. Robert Heideman, and the staff of Aquatic Eco-Systems, assembled a collection of photos and diagrams that helped make the illustrator's work possible. The staff at Agri Drain Corporation also helped with some illustrations. Jeff Persons, of Geo Source One, filled me in on the techniques involved in using geothermal ponds; John Longenecker, at Malibu Water Resources, offered information and useful suggestions about wind-pumping and aeration; Michael Caduto fielded many queries, and his book *Pond and Brook* was a reliable source of aquatic biology. Gail Vernazza managed to get it all skillfully word processed and introduced me to the wild world of e-mail and computers. Thanks to Helen Whybrow, who gave the project a green light, and editorial director Kermit Hummel, who drove the book home. Editors Ann Kraybill and Jennifer Thompson skillfully shepherded the project from manuscript to finished book, and Frank Fretz's illustrations unify and animate a wide variety of topics. And finally, to Jonathan Matson, for his business savvy and encouragement.

Introduction

The book you're holding is the result of my frustration at not finding a comprehensive source of all those nuggets of information essential to understanding constructed ponds. In my office I've got 20 feet of bookshelves full of aquaculture publications, and when I want to refresh my memory about pH, check out a new topic such as waterborne illnesses, or simply need a nuts-and-bolts cheat sheet, I usually wind up stranded behind a pile of books, magazines, catalogs, and clippings on the floor, with the computer spewing out sheets of interesting but not necessarily reliable information. Not a great way to access data.

Earth Ponds A to Z is my solution to that problem. The first two Earth Ponds books, and a video, have helped more than 90,000 people with their pond projects, but until now there hasn't been a basic, practical encyclopedia of ponds. This book thoroughly covers the two essentials of ponds—water and structure—providing comprehensive definitions and descriptions, often with helpful illustrations. Additional, essential topics include aquaculture techniques, leak detection and repair, animal attraction and control, regulatory issues, and more. Everything, in fact, from acid rain to zooplankton. Many pond builders and aquaculture professionals were consulted during the preparation of the book, and research was extensive. My objective was to create a book that covers the entire spectrum of ponds, in a new way in relation to the first two books.

There's been a revolution in pond use over the past quarter century. Natural ponds, earthen ponds, recreational ponds, impoundments, water gardems, silt pools, fish ponds—people call them all kinds of names today; even the venerable old "farm pond" gets an occasional mention, as it should, for spawning this new generation of reservoirs. Did I overlook irrigation pond, hydro pond, geothermal and solar pond, wastewater treatment pond, and constructed wetland?

A generation ago inland aquaculture was just a mom-and-pop blip on the economic radar. Today fish farms supply supermarkets with trout, catfish, carp, tilapia, crawfish, and shrimp, racking up more than $700 million in annual sales. The $800 million water garden business is growing 10 to 15 percent a year. And what country home is complete without a water garden or a recreational pond? New and old ponds are being used to relieve drought and even supply drinking water for homes without wells. One of the most recent innovations involves using ponds as a source of thermal energy for household heating and cooling, cutting energy costs as much as 50 percent.

Interest in ponds has never been higher. Drought, water quality, energy: Ponds offer potential solutions to some of our greatest challenges. They also offer aesthetic pleasure, recreation, and financial rewards. With a copy of *Earth Ponds A to Z* on your shelf, you'll have a quick, reliable, up-to-date database for the pond issues you want to tackle.

Earth Ponds A to Z

Acid Rain

Acidified precipitation results from coal-burning industrial processes, automobile combustion, and other sources. More accurately termed *acid fallout* or *deposition,* this type of pollution also involves dust particles and gases that can travel long distances downwind. Acid fallout can damage human-made materials (fabrics, paints, metals, stone structures) and plant and animal life. Acid rain is especially damaging to lakes and ponds. Bodies of water at high altitudes, downwind of coal-burning plants and other combustion sources, are especially vulnerable because thin soils in the surrounding watershed cannot buffer the acidic fallout. Thousands of lakes and ponds in North America, Europe, and Scandinavia have been rendered sterile by acid rain. The result: no fish, few insects, and water crystal clear and dead.

By the early 1990s the U.S. government mandated emissions reductions under the Clean Air Act, and acid rain began to drop off. Although many lakes and ponds became less acidic, recent studies show that a significant amount are still suffering from the effects of earlier pollution, as well as ongoing acid fallout. Plant and aquatic life have not recovered, and many scientists feel it may be decades before recovery begins.

Where ponds and lakes do suffer from the effects of acid fallout, it may be possible to improve water quality by raising the pH. This is usually done by adding agricultural limestone to the water and/or surrounding watershed. A pH of between 4.9 and 6.5 is considered "normal." In large bodies of water, liming costs may be prohibitive; studies also show that the effect of liming may be short lived and require periodic supplements.

Pond owners concerned about potential acidification should check pH levels throughout the year. pH can change dramatically depending on precipitation rates, wind flow patterns, and time of year. In the North spring snowmelt often releases accumulated acid fallout in a concentrated spike, which may result in fish-kills and other damage. Limestone spread on the ice prior to snowmelt may help neutralize this surge of acidity.

See *Limestone, pH, Water Conditioners,* and *Water Tests.*

Acid Water

pH levels below 5 are generally considered unhealthy to fish life and aquatic productivity. Acid water may be the result of one or more factors: acid precipitation; acidic soils; peat, runoff, or leachate from pine trees and other evergreens (needles, bark, lignin); and low exchange of fresh water. Acidic ponds are often found at high elevations downwind of fossil-fuel-burning power plants. Brown water is often a sign of high acid levels, due to runoff from conifers.

See *Brown Water.*

Acre-Foot

A unit of measurement used to quantify pond water volume. An acre-foot is the equivalent of 1 surface acre covered with 1 foot of water, 1/2 acre covered with 2 feet, and so forth. There are 325,851 gallons in each acre-foot. The U.S. Department of Agriculture (USDA) publishes a map of the United States that helps pond builders judge how large a drainage area is required to fill each acre-foot. For example, a pond with a 5-acre-foot capacity in central Missouri requires a 40-acre watershed. In western Washington State the same-sized pond needs just 1 acre.

See *Appendix A.*

Aeration

A healthy dissolved oxygen (DO) level is essential for aquatic life as well as the decomposition of animal waste products, organic matter, and decaying plant life. In ponds and lakes with insufficient oxygen, fish-kills are likely, and so is the accumulation of organic waste—which can lead to problems with algae, disease, and a further reduction in oxygen content. Ponds with little or no exchange of fresh water, shallow bottoms, fish overstocks, or high nutrient loads are all vulnerable to problems with low dissolved oxygen content.

How do you know your pond needs supplementary oxygen? DO monitoring can be done with chemical tests or digital meters. Water should be sampled at the surface, midlevel, and bottom. Five to 8 parts per million (ppm) is considered a healthy reading. Lower readings usually mean trouble. Ponds will often be stratified, with satisfactory readings at the surface and low oxygen levels on the bottom. Aeration systems are usually installed to raise DO levels, ideally at a uniform level throughout the pond. Aeration can be accomplished in a number of ways, from relatively simple infusions of fresh water to mechanical or compressed-air systems. One of the simplest ways to boost oxygen levels is to aerate the water by adding a flow of fresh water. Water pumped from a stream or other source can be splashed into a pond or run down a waterfall, enhancing oxygen content. Well water added to a pond may be low in oxygen, however; it should be tested and, if necessary, aerated.

Oxygen levels can also be raised by agitating water already in the pond. Splashing the water at surface level increases oxygen content in a localized area. Splash aerators are usually designed to float on the surface. Fountain aerators combine splash aeration with decorative aesthetics and are often used as landscaping elements, on golf courses, in water gardens, and near public buildings. Paddle-wheel aerators, often powered by tractors, were one of the earliest mechanical aeration systems, often used by fish farmers to counteract a fish-kill due to low oxygen. Splash aeration systems are particularly good in emergencies when oxygen levels need to be raised quickly. The problem with splash systems is that they affect a relatively small surface area and can raise water temperatures to unhealthy levels during summer days. They also speed up evaporation.

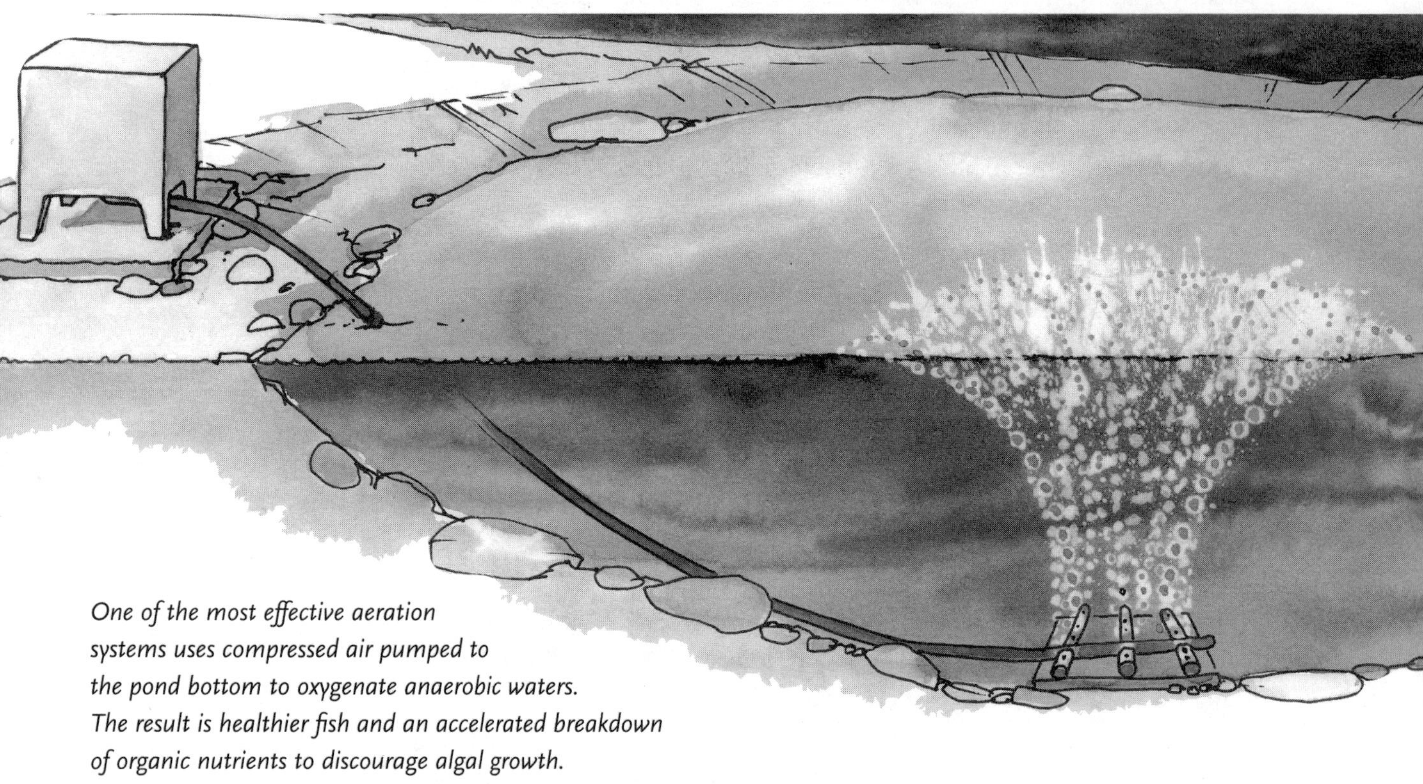

One of the most effective aeration systems uses compressed air pumped to the pond bottom to oxygenate anaerobic waters. The result is healthier fish and an accelerated breakdown of organic nutrients to discourage algal growth.

One of the most effective and economical aeration systems uses compressed air rather than agitation to increase dissolved oxygen levels. Air, or sometimes pure oxygen, is pumped to the bottom of the pond, where it bubbles to the surface in one or more columns of aerated water. Compressed-air systems can be especially helpful near the bottom where low DO prevents decomposition of organic sediment and doesn't support fish. Compressed-air systems are generally less power hungry than splash aerators and don't require an electrical line running through the water. An efficient compressed-air system can often help eliminate algal blooms by stimulating a healthy population of zooplankton and reducing the nutrient load. (In some situations, however, enhanced circulation may actually stimulate algal blooms.) Bubblers are also considered effective at removing gases such as ammonia and carbon dioxide, which harm fish. They help destratify the water, creating more uniform temperatures and oxygen levels. In some cases, such as raising trout, which require cold temperatures throughout the summer, destratifying temperatures may be undesirable. Fish growers often prefer bubblers to splash systems because of their efficiency, and because they create less noise, which can disrupt breeding.

In areas where electric power is unavailable, wind- or photovoltaic-powered aerators are often used. Wind and photovoltaic systems can be adapted to power splash aerators or bubblers.

See *Diffuser, Oxygen, Paddle-Wheel Aerator, Water Circulator, Waterfall,* and *Windpumps.*

Alga

In the beginning there was alga, the most primitive form of plant life and the foundation for the subsequent evolution of plants and animals. It was alga that created the earliest forms of oxygen, during photosynthesis, and alga that provided food for fish and other aquatic life. Tough and tenacious, alga will spring up in just about any form of water, from puddles to drinking wells, and it's even capable of growing on trees. Alga has adapted to fresh and salt water, and one of its favorite mediums is the freshwater pond. Most pond owners, however, are not overjoyed to find the first algal bloom in a new pond or a clump of pond scum rising during the first warm days of spring. It usually means trouble.

There are several basic forms of algae: the single-celled planktonic type, which can turn a pond pea soup green (or cappuccino brown); the filamentatious strands that can move through the water like ghostly fish; and more advanced types such as chara and nitella, which take root in the pond bed and colonize the water with their stringy green tentacles. (Some pond owners actually do fertilize algae to nourish certain species of fish.)

Aside from their life-giving properties, which include producing oxygen and food, algae can adversely affect water, particularly in ponds designed for human use. Algal blooms can clog piping, tangle up fishing lines, discourage swimming, create mosquito breeding areas, spoil landscape aesthetics, and be toxic to pets, wildlife, and livestock that drink the water. Algae can also cause rashes and diarrhea in swimmers.

Eliminating or controlling algae is often one of the pond owner's primary tasks. Like all plants, alga thrives on nutrients, and reducing sources of nitrogen and phosphorous discourages growth. Older ponds plagued by algal problems often benefit from dredging to eliminate the sedimentary source of nutrients as well as the alga itself and improve oxygen levels in the water. Maintaining a healthy exchange of fresh water helps infuse the water with dissolved oxygen, which accelerates decomposition of nutrients. Mechanical aeration can further improve oxygen levels. Ponds with deep, cool water and steep edges discourage plant growth. Natural biological controls can also discourage or eliminate algae. Grass carp (where permitted) are used by some pond owners to control algae, as are crawfish and various strains of nutrient-digesting bacteria. Nontoxic dyes can be used to shade the water, cutting off photosynthesis. Chemical algaecides offer algal control, although they may kill off fish and other aquatic life as well as damage the downstream watershed.

In general, pond owners designing for wildlife and wetland features are more tolerant of algae than those looking for more recreational benefits.

See *Aeration, Algaecides, Biological Aquatic Plant Management, Dye, Muskgrass, and Rakes.*

Algaecides

Chemical treatment for control and elimination of algae. Copper sulfate is one of the original algaecides and is still used by some pond owners to control both single-celled and filamentatious algae. Although it can be dramatically effective, results are usually temporary and often have lethal effects on nontarget organisms (fish, frogs, and the like) as well as contaminating sediments. More sophisticated formulations have been developed to treat specific algal species, and weeds, with less lethal side effects.

Algaecides work by inhibiting photosynthesis, cell development, and nitrogen uptake. The effectiveness of algaecides may depend on pH. Ponds with high alkalinity often need a higher dose. Some algal species are more sensitive to control than others, blue-green being easiest to quell.

Some algaecides are Environmental Protection Agency (EPA) approved for use in fish culture ponds; others should not be used in ponds accessible to fish, animals, or for recreation, irrigation, spraying, and the like. Depending on local regulations, algaecide application may or may not be legal, or may require a license. Be sure to read the labels, and check with regional authorities. Nonchemical algal and weed controls, as well as other water conditioners, are also available.

See *Bacteria, Barley Straw, Biological Plant Management, Dye,* and *Water Conditioners.*

Alkalinity

Alkalinity generally indicates the ability of water to neutralize, or buffer, acid conditions. (Water above 7 on the pH scale is considered alkaline, or basic.) Waters with a strong natural buffering capacity are often associated with soft rocks such as limestone. Because extremely acidic waters can be unhealthy for fish or other aquatic organisms, pond owners may wish to increase alkalinity. This can be done with the addition of agricultural limestone, sodium bicarbonate, or other chemicals. The effectiveness of buffering additives will depend on the hardness or softness of the water. Aeration can also help raise alkaline levels. Healthy decomposition of organic nutrients, which is beneficial to pond water quality, is usually improved by maintaining good alkaline levels. Keep in mind that raising alkaline levels may increase aquatic productivity to the point of stimulating unwanted aquatic vegetation, and raising it too high can prevent calcium from being available to growing fish.

See *Hard Water, Limestone,* and *Soft Water.*

Ammonia

A compound of nitrogen and hydrogen that builds up in water primarily from fish waste and in excessive levels can be toxic to fish and other aquatic animals. Ammonia toxicity will depend on amount of protein waste, pH, and temperature. Ammonia levels can be determined using test strips and other water-testing equipment.

See *Water Tests.*

Anti-Seep Collars

Underground pond piping is prone to seepage around the outside of the pipe, especially in overflow and drain systems buried in an embankment. This can cause significant leakage and even lead to dam failure. Anti-seep collars perpendicular to the pipe help prevent leakage. Collars vary from plastic gasketed fittings manufactured to fit various pipe sizes, to homemade plywood or iron collars. Plywood (nonarsenic marine grade) anti-seep collars should fit snugly around the pipe; seams are often coated with roofing tar to create a tight seal. Iron pipe collars are often welded. Collars usually work best when they match pipe materials.

Underground pond drains and spillways are vulnerable to leakage around the outside of the pipe. Anti-seep collars prevent these leaks.

The USDA recommends that anti-seep collars extend a minimum of 24 inches into the fill. If the dam is less than 15 feet high, one anti-seep collar at the centerline of the fill is enough. For higher dams, two or more collars should be evenly spaced between the fill centerline and the upstream connection to the riser, or hood inlet.

In my experience, omitting anti-seep collars is one of the principal causes of pond leaks and erosion.

See *Leaks.*

Anti-Vortex Device

A fitting at the top of a pipe spillway inlet that prevents overflowing water from spiraling around and causing erosion. Also known as a *splitter.*

See *Trash Guard.*

Aquatic Plants

Ponds are often a rich medium for plant growth, which may or may not be appreciated, depending on the owner's plans. Aquatic plants belong in three categories: submerged (underwater), emergent (underwater roots and stem, above-surface foliage and flowers), and shoreline (moist-soil loving). Water gardeners often cultivate all types of aquatic plants, and not only for their looks. Many submerged plants add oxygen to the water and filter nutrients, which improves water quality. Both submerged and emergent plants can provide shelter and food for fish, as well as harbor insects, which also sustain fish. Shoreline plants are attractive to birds as well as the pond owner.

Many of the plants that water gardeners intentionally introduce will volunteer in larger ponds. Depending on the owner's aim, these plants, and many more, may not be welcome. In larger ponds filamentatious algae and invasive aquatic plants may be difficult to control. Eventually, eutrophication results.

In some larger ponds aquatic growth is welcome. Constructed wetlands and ponds designed to attract waterfowl, and wildlife need plenty of plant life to succeed. Aquatics ranging from submerged coontail to emergent arrowhead and moist-soil cattails supply food, cover, and duck blinds. Often these plants are deliberately cultivated and encouraged by pond design.

The bottom line: Pay attention to the plant life in your pond and the kind of water quality you want. The correct aquatics (or absence of them) can make all the difference.

See *Invasive Exotic Plants, Moist-Soil Management,* and various aquatic plant varieties.

Aquifer

A permeable subterranean geological formation that stores and transports groundwater. Water enters an aquifer by surface water infiltration and is stored in sand, gravel, or layers of rock. A seam in the aquifer may allow water to reach the surface, especially water under pressure. A well drilled into an aquifer may yield flowing water if sufficiently pressurized (artesian well). Aquifers are also a source of well water that is to be pumped to the surface. Well water is liable to be low in dissolved oxygen, requiring aeration if used for raising fish. Although difficult to predict, occasionally a pond dug in an aquifer will release water from storage and adversely affect neighboring water sources.

See *Well.*

Arrowhead

An emergent aquatic plant with arrow-shaped leaves, similar to water plantain. Favored in wildlife ponds as a waterfowl attractant because its foliage and roots are edible. Rhizomes produce edible tubers relished by waterfowl, hence the plant's common name, duck potato. Its potential invasiveness and status as a beaver and muskrat attractant make it unwelcome in many recreational ponds.

See *Biological Plant Management* and *Invasive Exotic Plants.*

This aquatic plant is used for shoreline landscaping, water gardens, and to attract waterfowl. Caution: may be invasive.

Auger

A large spiral bit used as soil bore to determine the quality of soil, presence of rocks or stone, and water table. These rotating screwlike devices may be manually operated or motor driven. Manual soil augers offer a convenient, portable, low-budget way to test the soil in a potential pond site.

There are two types of soil auger: the pigtail auger, which has a spiral bit similar to the smaller carpenter's tool; and the bucket auger, with a cylindrical bore for extracting soil samples. Soil augers are useful in sampling soil profile, composition, and clay content, as well as in finding water. Soil augers are available with threaded extensions for deep probing.

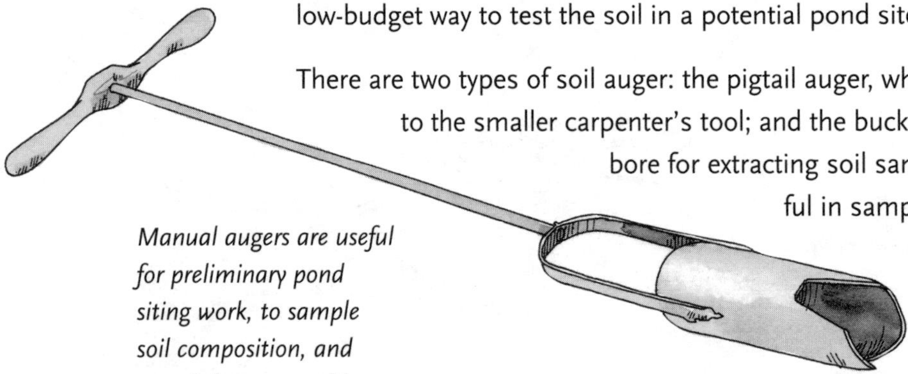

Manual augers are useful for preliminary pond siting work, to sample soil composition, and reveal the water table.

See *Backhoe* and *Test Pits.*

Backhoe

An excavating machine or attachment consisting of a hinged scoop connected to a mechanical arm that digs by being drawn back toward the machine. Most

Backhoes are often used in the critical first stage of pond siting: digging test pits.

backhoes operate on rubber tires, which confines their access to unobstructed, unflooded terrain. They're especially useful in pond construction during the siting phase, to dig test pits to check soil quality and water table, and can also be used to dig small excavated ponds. Backhoe attachments are available for tractors. They can also be useful for small-pond cleanouts, dredging along a pond shore, sediment pools, and repairs to eroded inflows and overflows.

See *Test Pits* and *Soil Tests.*

Bacteria

Under the right circumstances, live bacteria can be used in ponds to help reduce oxygen demand and nutrient loads—phosphorous, organic sludge, animal wastes—which in turn helps control algae. Aquatic management suppliers formulate blends of concentrated bacterial cultures that are introduced into lakes, ponds, and fish culture tanks. These bacterial strains proliferate when introduced and eat up the sludge, animals wastes, and so on. Bacteria work best when pH, temperature, alkalinity, and oxygen levels are favorable. Manufacturers' directions specify optimal water conditions and usually caution against using in cold water, which inhibits bacterial activity. Recent studies show that adding a carbon source (such as sugar or corn starch) to the water helps activate bacteria.

See *Water Conditioners.*

Barley Straw

A new method of controlling filamentatious alga ("pond scum") uses barley straw submerged along pond shorelines. The rotting straw produces hydrogen peroxide as it decomposes, which kills the alga. Barley straw has proved more effective than wheat, hay, or grass and is usually anchored underwater in shallow net bags. To be most effective, pond temperatures should be 40 degrees F or more, with good dissolved oxygen levels and water circulation. The recommended application rate is approximately 30 pounds of straw per 1/4 acre. Straw works best if applied early in the season and should be reapplied roughly every six months, and old straw removed. Shoreline applications of straw have also been used traditionally to help clarify turbid waters. Barley straw is available from aquatic suppliers and water gardening outfits.

See *Alga*.

Beach

Ponds used for recreational purposes often benefit from the addition of a sand beach. A well-designed beach offers comfortable access to the water for swimmers, a shallow wading area for children, and, if large enough, picnic and sunbathing areas. Beach sand is also effective at mulching aquatic plants that would otherwise obstruct recreational activities. In an especially weedy pond,

A layer of washed sand spread over a sheet of porous geotextile fabric creates a fine swimming beach and suppresses weeds.

the beach may be the only decent swimming area. For safety reasons the limits of the swimming area may be marked by a string of floats.

There are several criteria for a good beach. The approach to the water and submerged area should be gently sloped (4 to 1 or flatter). Steep sandy areas are vulnerable to erosion, and swimming areas that drop off abruptly can be dangerous for children and novice swimmers. If the beach can be sited at the northern end of the pond, orientation to sun and water is ideally combined. The beach and swimming area should not be close to drop-inlet pipes, aeration equipment, or other structures that might cause injury. Shoreland where springs or inflow channels run into the pond should also be avoided, as well as electrical lines running into the water. If the beach area includes some shade trees, all the better, although deep-rooted trees should not be planted in a dam.

It's possible to dump a truckload or more of sand directly on the beach area, but erosion is likely to wash it farther into the water before long. A more durable beach can be created by digging out the area to be covered to a depth of about 6 inches, lining the ground with plastic or filter fabric, and then adding the sand. In existing ponds, water can be drawn down to expose the submerged beach area, which can then be excavated, lined, and covered with sand. If there's any concern that digging into the pond bed will cause leaks, the bottom should be left undisturbed and covered with liner material and sand. The sand itself should be a washed masonry type, which is preferable to quarried sand containing organic material; this causes turbidity in the water. A beach area above the waterline approximately 20 feet wide by 10 feet deep is considered by many pond owners an adequate size, with something comparable in the water. Beaches that get a lot of traffic may benefit from being larger.

Beavers

Beavers and ponds are linked in numerous ways. Beavers are the original pond engineers, and when humans decide to build their own reservoirs, they're using similar basic techniques—excavation, dam building, and spillway construction. But aside from sharing pond-building ambitions and methods, humans and beavers may find themselves in conflict. Often the pond sites that people choose are near wetlands that support beavers, and these new ponds attract beavers looking for habitat. When beavers start damming spillways to manipulate water levels, building lodges, and cutting down trees, people object (unless they're pleased to have created a wildlife refuge). Beavers carry diseases such as giardiasis and tularemia, which can infect humans. Plugged spillways can lead to breached dams and flooded ponds. Felled trees may not be part of the landowner's landscaping plans. Beaver removal may be necessary, and it can be attempted in different ways.

Beavers can be live-trapped in a pond and then removed to another area, sometimes with the assistance of local wildlife officials, the state natural resources agency, or the like. Where permitted, lethal trapping is another option, and some pond owners find a local trapper interested in setting the traps and harvesting the pelts. Whether you have someone do the trapping for you, or do it yourself, make sure it's permitted by your state natural resources agency. Both live and lethal traps are available through sporting outfitters and other outdoor organizations. Some pond owners prefer to shortcut the trapping option and shoot the beavers, but again, this should be considered as a last resort, and must be legal.

Many pond owners prefer more benign methods of beaver removal. One of the best ways to begin is to make the pond unattractive to the animals. Because beavers need trees for food and building materials, people sometimes wrap tree trunks with wire-mesh fencing to protect them. Chemical repellents can also be

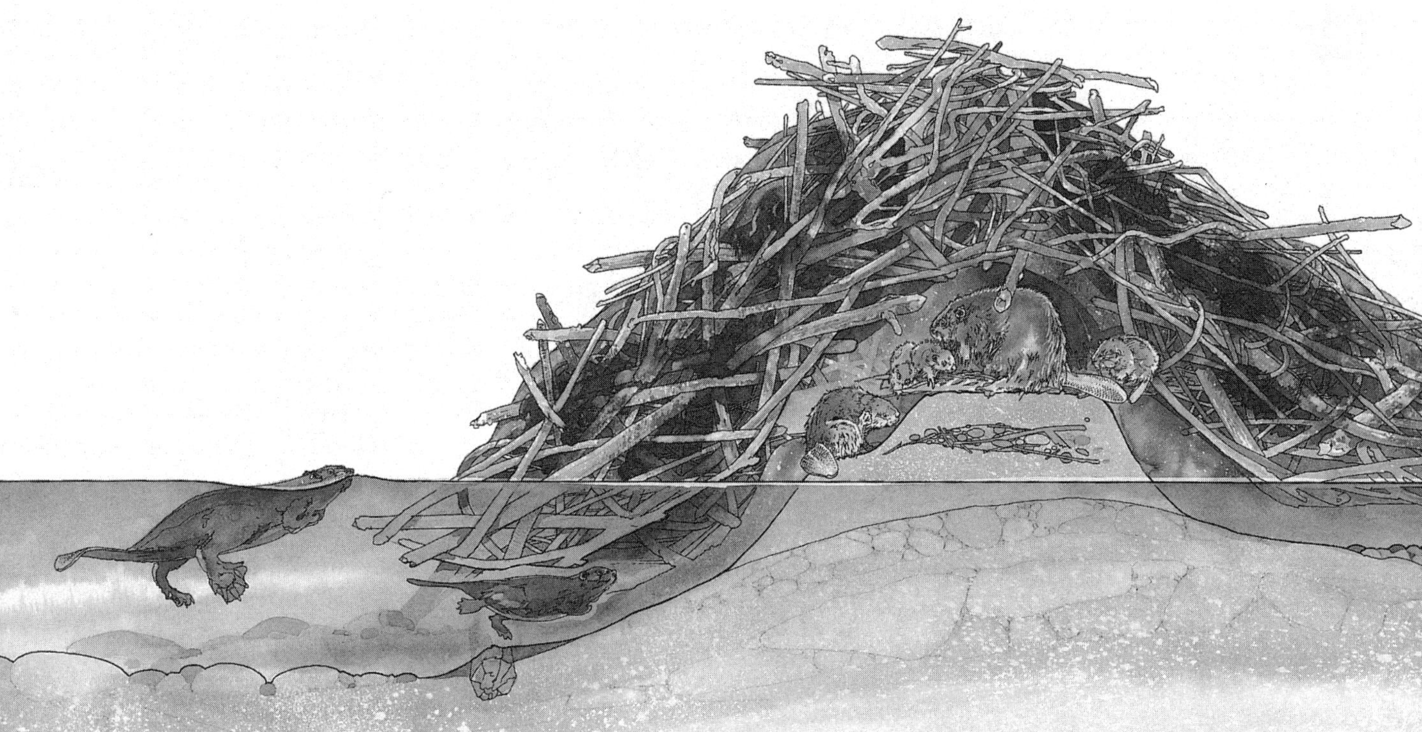

Wildlife pond owners often welcome beavers, although others may be troubled by plugged pipes and spillways, felled trees, and contaminated water. The potential for beaver problems is one of the best reasons I know for avoiding wetland pond sites.

applied to trees to deter beavers; applying these repellents to beaver "scent mounds" around the pond may also discourage the animals.

Researchers have discovered that beavers are instinctively attracted to the sound of running water, which is why they like to plug up spillways and overflow channels. Spillway siphon systems have been designed with submerged inlets to eliminate these sounds and discourage the beavers. Baffles and other protective devices can be used to restrict access to inlet pipes and overflow channels. When beavers dam up spillway channels, tearing the dams out may result in temporary success; often, however, the beavers are back soon to rebuild. It may be more effective to breach the dam with perforated piping at the desired water level, which the beavers have a hard time plugging up. Protective steel grilles can be built to protect vertical inlets from being plugged, and fencing is sometimes used to cordon off inlet pipes and spillway canals. Electric fencing around vulnerable piping may also be effective.

See *Beaver Baffles, Beaver Repellents,* and *Tree Wrap.*

Beaver Baffles

A *beaver baffle* or *baffler* is a generic term that can be applied to any exclusionary device designed to keep beavers from plugging pond outlets or building dams that might lead to flooding. Baffles include drainage pipes inserted through beaver dams, spillway systems designed to prevent plugging or damming, and fencing devices mounted on or near spillways.

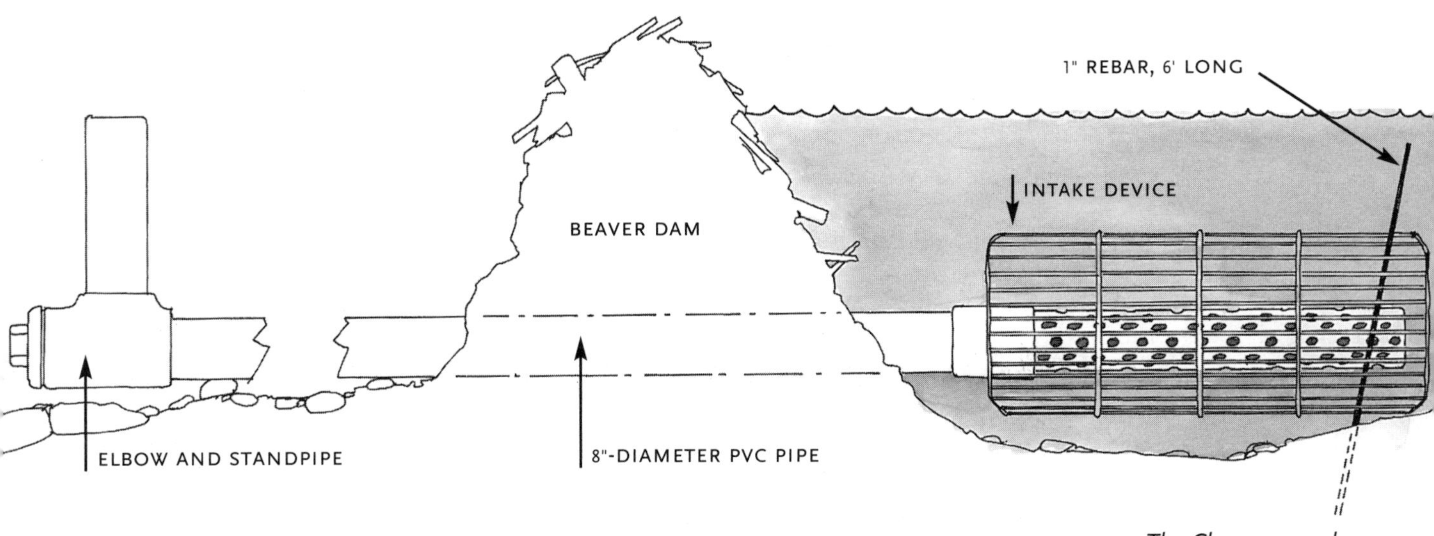

The Clemson pond leveler is one of many baffles designed to prevent beaver damage. The leveler uses a steel cage to protect the inlet pipe against plugging. An optional standpipe (left) enables the pond manager to maintain a predetermined water level or drain the pond. Designed by Gene W. Wood, Clemson University.

Beavers often build dams across earth-cut spillways to increase pond depth. Removing these dams usually provokes more dam building, leading to a frustrating cycle of construction–destruction that may end in a needlessly lethal "solution." A better remedy involves compromise. Tear down the dam to an acceptable water level, and securely install one or more perforated plastic pipes, so that when the beavers rebuild the dam, the baffles will keep the pond drained. Drop inlets, another beaver target, even when equipped with a trash guard, often invite plugging. Siphon spillway systems with submerged inlets are not as attractive to beavers as the water level drains and are less likely to be plugged. Beavers are attracted to the sound of running water, which they rush to plug up. Submerged inlets are silent. Horizontal water-level culvert-type overflows are another beaver target, and a variety of baffles can be used to prevent damming. The entire area can be fenced off, the pipe can be fitted with a large trash guard (often fastened to a chain used to pull away dam-building material), or an electric fence can be installed around the pipe. Other baffles include the Clemson pond leveler, which uses a protective cage around a horizontal water-level spillway pipe.

See *Beavers* and *Beaver Repellents.*

Beaver Repellents

Beavers taking up lodging in or near human-made ponds can do significant damage to surrounding trees and shrubs, in addition to the pond structure itself. Strategies to deter beavers from building dams and plugging spillways include fencing and devices that thwart the dam-building process. Natural and synthetic chemicals are also used as beaver repellents. These liquid compounds can be painted or sprayed on trees and shrubs, including the foliage of young trees, roses, and so on. As of this writing, the only EPA-approved commercial beaver repellent is Ropel, which is sprayed or painted on plants, giving the treated surface a bitter taste. Applications wash off in two to three months. Some experts in beaver management, however, find that big-game repellents—which include sulfurous/putrid egg ingredients—work better, although they are not EPA approved. Another effective tree treatment is reported to be a combination of latex- or oil-based paint mixed with masonry sand; apparently beavers do not like the taste of sand. The paint can be color-matched to the trees, so your woods won't look like a scene from *Fantasia.* Other recommendations include the scat of otters, industrial sandpaper wrapped around the bottom 4 feet of the trees (although the dark color may heat up in the sun and damage the tree), dogs, and a combination of large-animal repellents and eucalyptus oil. In the end, fencing may be the best tree protection.

See *Beaver Baffles* and *Tree Wrap.*

Bentonite

Naturally occurring colloidal clay with particles that absorb water and swell to 20 times their original size. During hydration, bentonite becomes a dense mass with low hydraulic conductivity. When applied to porous soil, it creates an effective water-retaining liner. Frequently used to leakproof drilled wells, bentonite is also used in leaky ponds to reduce soil porosity and seepage. Bentonite has to be correctly applied to the dry pond bed to be effective and is usually disked in with a tractor or rototiller. It is also available incorporated in geotextile liner mats. Bentonite's chief shortcoming is its tendency to cause turbidity in pond water. That and its greasy texture make it unsuitable in many recreational ponds.

See *Clay* and *Liners.*

Berm

A mound of earth built up to deflect runoff or floodwater. Berms are sometimes used around a pond to protect against flooding or to direct overflow. Similar to embankment and levee, but smaller. (Also used to refer to a graded flat strip of land. Confusing, eh?)

See *Embankment.*

Biological Aquatic Plant Management

Algae and some invasive aquatic plants can be controlled without toxic chemicals by introducing bacteria, certain types of fish, aquatic animals, and waterfowl. Bacterial solutions of beneficial microorganisms can improve the biodegradation of sediment, as well as reduce availability of nitrogen and phosphorous to feed algae and plant life. Such bioaugmentation can lower ammonia and nitrite levels, improve oxygen levels, and lead to an increase in zooplankton, which feed on algae. Bacterial solutions require suitable water conditions, including favorable pH, temperature, alkalinity, and oxygen. Water tests may be needed to determine a pond's qualification for bioaugmentation.

Grass carp, crawfish, snails, geese, and ducks can be used as natural controls for aquatic plants. Effective use of these live controls will depend on pond conditions and may be regulated by state agencies. Keep in mind that introducing fish or other critters may have negative side effects as well, including increased turbidity and nutrient levels, fecal contamination, and damage to the pond structure.

See *Bacteria, Crawfish, Grass Carp, Snails,* and *Waterfowl.*

Biological Insect Pest Management

Considering the threat of the West Nile virus, mosquito control may be one of the pond manager's greatest challenges.

Ponds troubled by mosquitoes, black flies, and other insects may be improved with the implementation of biological management controls (integrated pest management, pond-style). Dragonflies and damselflies live around ponds and other water bodies, where they breed, lay their eggs, and develop from nymphs to adults. As nymphs and adults, they are superb fliers and voracious insect eaters, valued by pond owners for their ability to control mosquitoes. Pond owners with mosquito problems can augment the natural dragonfly population by purchasing dragonfly larvae from biological suppliers. Larvae should be released over the water in spring before the mosquito season gets underway. The town of Wells, Maine, is famous for its successful dragonfly mosquito control program.

Bats are another voracious insect eater, and ponds may be improved by adding bat houses. (Beware, however, that bats also eat dragonflies.) Bats can be encouraged to set up housekeeping near a pond by installing two or three bat houses per acre in the vicinity of the pond. The best location for a bat house is on a tree or structure with an eastern to southern exposure, about 12 to 15 feet in the air, with a clear flight path into the house. In trees, all branches below the bat house should be removed.

Mosquito larvae can be controlled by using a natural bacteria. "Mosquito dunks" consist of a solid formulation of *Bacillus thuringiensis* formed into a briquette that floats in water, and when mosquito larvae feed on the dissolving material, their digestive system breaks down, killing them. Each dunk treats about 100 square feet of water and lasts about 30 days. The dunks should be stocked prior to the onset of the mosquito season, when the larvae are first appearing. Mosquito dunks are more effective in ponds, vernal pools, and bird baths; they don't work as well in fragmented swampy areas where the larvae is widely dispersed. Mosquito dunks are EPA approved.

Mosquito larvae are also appetizing to goldfish and guppies and "annual" fish that appear in vernal pools and ponds. One particularly effective mosquito eater is the mosquito fish *(gambusia affinis)*, a versatile fish that can live in as little as 2 inches of warm water. This lover of mosquito larvae is native west of the Rockies, and U.S. Fish and Wildlife regulations prohibit import in the east because of concerns about invasive non-native species. One useful fish native to the east is the mummichog, which is reputed to be effective at mosquito control and is sold by biological pest management suppliers.

Birds such as purple martins and swallows are also great insect eaters, but like bats, they too feast on dragonflies. If you're serious about mosquito control, dragonflies and mosquito dunks look like the best bets.

See *Mosquitoes.*

Biologist

Two kinds of professionally trained specialists can be helpful regarding pond issues: fisheries and aquatic biologists. For pond owners raising fish, questions regarding fish health, regional species preferences, stocking rates, and habitat can often be answered by fisheries biologists working for state fish and wildlife departments, university extension services, or private companies. Aquatic biologists may be able to help solve problems with water quality, invasive aquatic plants, and other pond issues. (A windmill dealer I know developed a unique method of improving water quality using wind-powered aeration while working with California state aquatic biologists.) Aquatic biologists may be located at state extension services, natural resource departments, as well as private outfits. Biologists with federal agencies such as the U.S. Fish and Wildlife Department and Environmental Protection Agency may also be able to offer helpful information and assistance. Your tax dollars are paying for these professionals; why not use them?

Bird Damage Control

Owners may find that their ponds have become the destination of waterfowl and other birds. Geese and ducks may choose ponds as layover spots on their migratory flyways or as nesting areas to raise their young. Herons, kingfishers, cormorants, and other species target ponds with fish and other aquatic animals to feed on. Although many pond owners welcome waterfowl and predatory birds and create habitats that encourage them, birds can have a negative effect on water quality. Geese, especially, can pollute swimming and drinking water, and their waste can foul shoreland areas. Once established, geese can be difficult to remove, and because they're a federally protected species (along with most other waterfowl and migratory birds), only a limited number can be killed during hunting season. Recently, dealing with intrusive birds has become a growing problem for pond managers. Bird populations have increased because of protective laws, decreases in hunting, loss of habitat to development, loss of predators, and expansive grassy landscaping.

Controlling bird damage will depend on the species of bird involved and the type of pond. Efforts to remove geese should begin as soon as they appear. The longer they stay, the more stubborn they become about leaving. Scare-away devices are sold by aquacultural suppliers, including mechanical noisemakers that can be regulated to discharge at varying intervals, pistols that shoot pyrotechnic devices, pyrotechnic shotgun shells, and recorded distress calls that may frighten off birds. Dead goose decoys are also used. Automated water spray

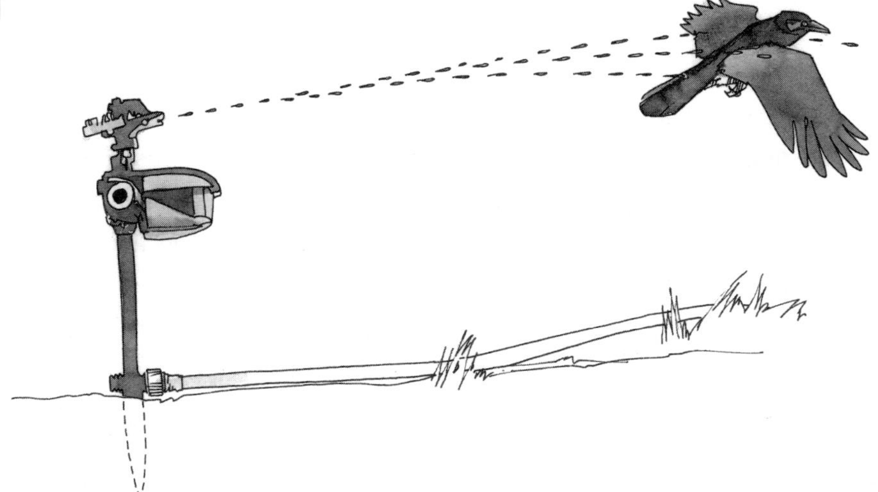

Nonlethal scare-away devices can be used to discourage unwanted birds and animals. The motion activated sprinkler (left) sprays short bursts of water, and the balloon with hungry eyes mimics predatory owls and hawks.

devices can be used to disturb birds without causing injury. Scarecrows, helium balloons, and inflatable owl faces can be set up around the pond, as well as strings of shiny Mylar tape. Dogs can also help frighten away geese, fences can keep geese from approaching a pond on foot, and nontoxic liquids make the grass distasteful. USDA specialists recommend that to be most effective, several methods need to be combined; also, scare-away devices should be repositioned regularly.

Predatory birds can be a serious threat to anyone raising fish. Professional fish farmers are often left with no alternative but to cover raceways and ponds with elaborate netting or wire grids, but the cost is usually justified by increased crops. Pond owners raising fish on a smaller scale will probably not want to incur the expense of netting, not to mention putting the entire pond behind bars. Less drastic protective measures involve altering the pond habitat to discourage birds such as herons and kingfishers. Deepening the edge area around the pond will make it difficult for herons to stalk fish in the shallows. Some pond owners also use an electric fence along the shore or float a string of buoys around the perimeter to interfere with wading birds. Kingfishers prefer an elevated perch to sit on and launch their attacks, so it may be helpful to remove trees from near the pond edge.

Habitat alteration and pond management can also help deter waterfowl. Removing islands and peninsulas eliminates protective refuges. In northern climates, allowing the pond to freeze over completely discourages overwintering. Vegetative cover and food plants in and around the pond should be eliminated. In some agricultural areas, this may require altering crop species and planting schedules. The USDA and state wildlife biologists offer information and on-site evaluation of bird control strategies.

One of the newest control techniques involves using model airplanes to scare off predatory birds—the Red Baron saves your bass.

Bottom Barriers

Bottom barriers are used to prevent the growth of aquatic plants on the pond bed. Like plastic laid down to kill weeds in a garden, a bottom barrier kills submerged plants by cutting off sunlight, as well as preventing new seeds from rooting. Bottom barriers are usually made of nonporous plastic of a durable mil and are UV resistant. Rubber, fiberglass screen, or nylon may also be used. Bottom barriers are often used in beach areas and covered with sand as extra protection against puncturing. They may also be installed in specific problem areas. Installation is most effective during pond construction, or drawdown, over areas where growth is not active or has been removed. Rocks or other anchoring objects are used to keep the barrier in place; keep in mind that weighting barriers down with soil creates a new medium for growth. Sediment accumulating on the barrier will eventually support vegetation, making barriers only temporarily effective. Deteriorating barrier material may become a problem over time. Suspended or floating vegetation will not be prevented.

Bridges

Pond inflow and outflow channels often require bridges for foot traffic, small vehicles (lawn mowers, garden tractors), or full-size cars and trucks. Pond bridges span the gamut from delicate teak arches to steel I-beams covered with hemlock planks. Bridges should be set on solid footings, with precautions taken to prevent erosion from undermining the foundation. Bridges should not hang so low over the water that they may snag passing debris and create a trash jam. Pond embankments sometimes serve as roads, with a spillway pipe running through the structure, making it, in effect, a bridge. Be sure these pipes or culverts are carefully protected to prevent crushing, with anti-seep collars to prevent erosion and dam/bridge failure. Bridges are also used as spans between shore and an island. Practical and aesthetically pleasing, bridges often add a dramatic element to a pond design.

Brimful Effect

A design feature that creates the appearance that water is close to the level of the surrounding shore, and the pond is "brimful" of water. In some cases this may be a fact, in other ponds more an illusion. Traditional USDA/Soil Conservation Service pond designs often used plans that incorporated several feet of freeboard (the vertical distance from water level to the top of the shore), especially in embankment ponds, as a safety precaution against flooding during high-precipitation events. This frequently produced ponds with a craterlike appearance, especially if the water level fell during dry weather. High freeboard, especially combined with steep slopes, also makes access to the water awkward and mowing difficult. Pond owners interested in aesthetic appearance, as well as a ramble close to the water's edge, may prefer the brimful effect.

The problem is that if you reduce the freeboard too much, the pond may be vulnerable to flooding. One way to decrease freeboard without increasing flood potential is to gradually feather the embankment slope down to the waterline and then increase the submerged basin slope to standard design criteria (roughly 3 to 1). It's also possible to oversize the spillway (channel or pipe), as

Steep freeboard can create an unattractive, awkward approach to the water. The brimful shoreline offers a more natural surround.

well as the emergency spillway, as an extra precaution against flooding. In ponds with small watersheds and inflows, freeboard may not be as critical.

See *Freeboard* and *Embankment*.

Brown Water

Ponds sometimes exhibit a vivid brown hue, which people often describe as tea or coffee colored. Although the water may not be especially turbid, transparency is reduced, as is algal growth. These ponds are often located in wooded areas and may have been excavated in soil containing peat, which contributes to the brown color and acidity. Other factors that can contribute to brown water include tannin from pine needles; bark and lignin; and iron deposits in the soil, which bacteria break down and release as orange residues and oily slicks often mistaken for petroleum spills. Brown water ponds are often found at high elevations where the water is acidy and there is little exchange of fresh water to dilute the effect. These waters may not be productive, due to lack of algae and diatoms, but are usually suitable for swimming.

See *Acid Water.*

Bulldozer

A construction vehicle with tracks and a front-end blade used for moving earth, rocks, tree stumps, and the like. Bulldozers are often used for pond construction, especially in embankment ponds where an earth dam is built to hold water. Wide tracks make it possible for bulldozers to work in wet areas, although they can bog down in extremely swampy sites, and operators have to be careful about keeping the area well drained. The weight of the machine distributed on wide tracks is also useful in dam construction, packing the soil efficiently, especially when built up in layers. Many ponds have been built with a single bulldozer, from site clearing to final grading, although it's often more effective to combine an excavator and a dozer, especially in extremely wet areas, where the impoundment is created mostly by excavation. More than

This versatile machine is often used in many stages of pond construction: site preparation, excavation, embankment construction, and final grading. Without pumping or drainage ditching, it's not as effective in extremely wet terrain.

one bulldozer has been lost forever during construction of a pond in a swampy site.

See *Excavator.*

Bypass Pipe

Ponds are sometimes sited where they require supplemental water, in addition to on-site springs and inflowing streams. Such a pond may be sited adjacent to a brook that is too large to run directly into the pond, because of the risk of erosion and siltation. Usually a bypass system consists of a pickup box or cistern in or adjacent to the stream, connected to a pipe that runs downhill from the stream to the pond. If the stream pickup cannot be sited at a higher elevation, then a pump may be needed. The intake pipe may have a foot valve to prevent running the cistern dry. In the North the pipe is usually buried below frost line to prevent freezing. A valve at the pipe outlet controls the flow. The cistern, box, or pool should be designed so that accumulated silt can be cleaned out periodically.

Cage Culture

An aquaculture method that uses cages to contain fish crops. Floating cages are often used, although they may be attached to piers and other structures. Cage culture is popular with pond farmers because it allows them to grow different sizes and species of fish in a single pond, and then harvest them efficiently. Growers must feed fish regularly and make sure fish are not overcrowded. Covered cages also protect fish from birds and aquatic predators. Some growers, however, complain that fish grown in cages are prone to injury from hitting the netting and structure, especially in overcrowded conditions.

Floating fish cages offer predator protection, and enable growers to isolate different species within the same pond.

Cattails *(Typha latifolia; T. angustifolia)*

Cattails are native to wetlands and can be an attractive plant feature. Caution: may be invasive.

Emergent aquatic plants that thrive in marshes and shallow pond areas. They are tall (3 to 9 feet) and noted for the furry brown spike of female flowers that gives them their name, as well as flat leaves that can be used for chair caning.

Roots, shoots, and flowers are edible and were harvested by Native Americans and colonists. The cattail provides food and habitat for wildlife (waterfowl, marsh birds, muskrats) and filters and purifies water. Pond owners often allow a patch of cattails to stand, for wildlife benefits. Clearly, this is an important wetland plant, although it can be invasive in shallow ponds and may need to be controlled before it colonizes the pond. Cutting off the stem before flowering, below the waterline, kills the plant.

See *Biological Aquatic Plant Management, Invasive Exotic Plants,* and *Reeds.*

Chemical Shading

See *Dye.*

Clay

A fine-grained earthy material essential for water retention in pond soils. The best pond sites have soils that include enough clay to hold water; lacking sufficient clay, pond soils can be made more leak resistant with the addition of a clay liner.

There are three soil types—sand, loam, and clay—and good pond soil is usually a blend of the three. Depending on the type of clay, and the percentage of other soil types and gravel, good pond soil will include approximately 10 to 20 percent clay, or more. Still, too much clay can create problems with water turbidity, and pond embankments built with pure clay can crack where exposed to air and sunlight. High-percentage clay does make good liner material, though.

Soil with a relatively low clay content can sometimes be improved using good compaction construction techniques. Bentonite, a special type of volcanic clay, is sometimes added to porous soil to improve water retention; it should be worked into the soil during pond construction. It may cause turbidity. Clay-caused turbidity problems can sometimes be offset with a protective covering of gravel, the addition of gypsum, or straw around the pond edges.

How do you know if your soil includes enough clay? Roll up a clump of moist soil in your hand and squeeze. If it holds together in a ball, you're likely to have good pond soil. Pure clay can be rolled up into "snakes," like modeling clay. If you want to get really technical, the USDA recommends (in Agriculture Handbook 590,

Ponds—Planning, Design, Construction) that "soils with at least 20 percent passing the No. 200 sieve, a Plasticity Index of more than 10 percent, and an undisturbed thickness of at least 3 feet do not have excessive seepage when the water depth is less than 10 feet." Another way to gauge clay content is to precipitate a soil sample. Screen a soil sample through 1/2-inch mesh to remove pebbles and gravel. Fill a glass jar one-third full with the soil sample, top off with water, and cap. (A 1-quart canning jar works well.) Shake it up and then set aside for 24 hours. The coarse sandy material will settle first, then silt, and finally clay. Measure the proportions of sand, silt, and clay. The top stratum of clay should comprise at least 20 percent. Keep in mind that clay content can vary throughout a pond site, and some areas may need additional clay. Sometimes a contractor will be able to distribute on-site clay throughout the pond bed so that porous areas are leakproofed.

From prehistoric times, clay has been an essential ingredient in building materials and industrial processes, as well as in agriculture. It seems fitting that it should also be a key ingredient in pond construction.

See *Barley Straw, Gypsum, Soil Tests,* and *Test Pits.*

Cleanout

As ponds age, they fill up with sediment and aquatic vegetation and generally take the journey to becoming a swamp known as *eutrophication.* To reverse this process and rejuvenate the pond, pond owners periodically clean out the basin. This usually involves hiring a contractor to dredge the pond. The cleanout process is best accomplished by first draining the pond (using a built-in drain, if available, or via siphon or pumping). If there is no drain to keep the pond empty, a pump may have to be run periodically to keep the pond from filling; cleanouts are best done in dry weather to minimize drainage problems. If fish are stocked, they should be harvested before the pond is drained. Frogs and salamanders will usually seek new habitat as the pond dries up, but there may be fatalities. Another potential casualty is the seal that lines the pond. If the pond was lined with clay, care should be taken not to destroy the seal; otherwise, it may have to be replaced. If the pond is lined with a plastic or fabric sheet, any damage will cause leaks. Even ponds that have no clay or sheet liners may lose their natural leakproofing during a cleanout, and may not hold water effectively until a new layer of sediment accumulates. Material from the cleanout should be removed far enough from the pond area to prevent damage to the shore due to crushing or erosion. Dredged material is usually trucked to a location where it can drain; it's then used to grade off uneven ground or sold as fill.

See *Excavator* and *Sedimentation.*

Compaction Testing

During the construction of a pond embankment, soil testing can be performed to determine soil density and moisture content. This is usually done on engineered ponds where a state and/or federal building permit is required. Embankments are often built in "lifts," or layers of compacted material one on top of the other. These layers can be compaction tested to make sure the embankment conforms to engineering standards and will hold the designed water load.

See *Embankment.*

Constructed Wetlands

Human-made wetlands are built to compensate for destroyed wetlands, as a part of mandatory government mitigation programs; they are also created to add new wetlands to the landscape, for numerous practical and aesthetic reasons. Constructed wetlands can be used for wastewater purification systems, flood control and groundwater recharge, erosion control, and wildlife and native plant habitat. They are also valued for aesthetic, recreational, and educational purposes. Often a constructed wetland will fulfill several of these functions simultaneously.

Recently wetlands have gained much attention as wastewater purification systems. Because of their unique combination of hydrology, soils, and plant life, wetlands have the capacity to purify contaminated water without the use of chemicals and related sewage plant equipment. It's been shown that constructed wetlands are capable of treating wastewater at a rate 10 times less expensively than conventional sewage systems.

Criteria for a constructed wetland include availability of water, topography, soils, property availability, and adjacent land use. For water treatment wetlands, proximity to the wastewater source is another consideration.

Design for a wastewater wetland must take into account volume of flow, composition of pollutants, shape, aquatic plants to be used, and spillway control structure. Because many of these wetland systems are designed for municipal wastewater treatment, government permitting is often required. Design assistance can usually be found at local, state, and federal levels, as well as from private organizations.

See *Wetlands.*

Construction Fabric

Various geotextile fabrics (synthetic and organic) may come into play during the construction or renovation of a pond. Waterproof fabrics can be used to prevent erosion in earthen spillways and on dam slopes, as well as reduce sedimentation from drainage areas around the pond. Woven mats allow plants to grow through the fabric, encouraging a soil stabilizing root system to develop at the same time disturbed soil is protected. Some are woven using organic fibers that will eventually decompose. Construction fabric can also be used as a foundation membrane to create a base for a sand beach.

See *Beach, Bottom Barriers, Erosion,* and *Silt Fence.*

Coontail *(Ceratophyllum demersum)*

A submerged aquatic plant that creates good insect habitat and protection for young fish, coontail is often used in wildlife ponds to attract ducks, geese, swans, and marsh birds. It also attracts muskrats, however, which can create a pest problem in recreational ponds. Because these plants tend to be invasive, recreational pond owners usually prefer to do without.

See *Invasive Exotic Plants.*

Coontail is a widespread aquatic plant used by water gardeners but considered a nuisance weed by recreational pond owners. Also called Hornwort.

Copper Sulfate

A chemical compound long used as an algaecide and fungicide, although it's not as popular as it once was with pond owners because of restrictive regulations and knowledge of its damaging side effects. Copper sulfate was an old standby for eliminating algae as well as the organism that causes swimmer's itch. (Copper is a potent toxin; farmers learned they could throw an old automobile radiator in a pond to suppress algae.) Used in granular form or spray, copper sulfate has been found to be most effective in water 60 degrees F or warmer. In addition to cold temperatures, high alkalinity (pH) will diminish its performance. Copper sulfate is most effective when used in the early stages of an algal bloom.

Copper sulfate's shortcomings and collateral damage outweigh its usefulness. It kills not only algae but also fish, animals, and invertebrates (not to mention the potential for harm to humans using the pond or living downstream). Dissolved oxygen levels are reduced because of the elimination of photosynthesizing plants, and zooplankton are killed off, wiping out natural algal predators. In fact, effectiveness is relatively brief, with a rebound effect that eventually hits the pond with even more severe algal blooms. In most states, use of copper sulfate is restricted and requires a permit.

Core Trench

Pond embankments are vulnerable to leakage at the base of the dam, especially if native material above the base is pervious sand or gravel over a clay foundation. To prevent seepage through the seam between the clay and the gravel/sand or other fill, a core trench is dug in the dam foundation. This trench is excavated in impervious material along the centerline of the dam and packed with layers of clay high enough into pervious embankment material to prevent leakage. The core trench, also known as a *cutoff* or *key,* extends into the abutments as far as needed to prevent leakage.

See *Embankment.*

Crawfish

North American freshwater crawfish (or *crayfish, crawdads,* or *crabs*) inhabit ponds, lakes, and rivers across the country. There are more than 400 species of crawfish, ranging in size from the large red swamp variety found in the South to the smaller virilis and papershell of higher latitudes. Red swamp crawfish are trapped in the wild and raised commercially for food; smaller varieties are also trapped and raised, but more often to be used as bait.

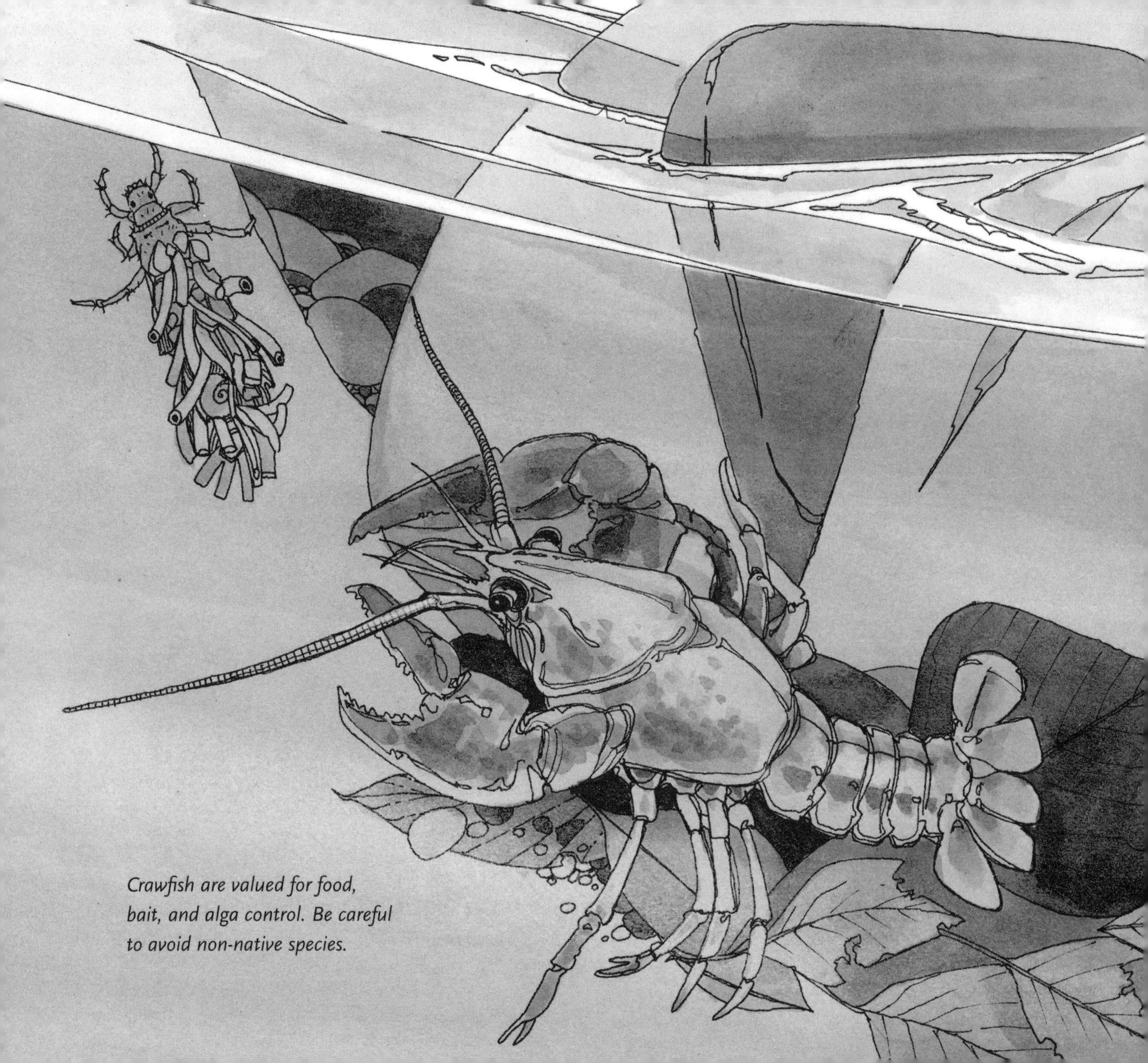

Crawfish are valued for food, bait, and alga control. Be careful to avoid non-native species.

Crawfish can find their way into ponds naturally or be intentionally introduced. In addition to being used as food and bait, crawfish may be valuable to pond owners for their scavenging instincts. These omnivorous invertebrates feed on larvae, insects, and amphibians, and also pond bed detrius and algae. Their talent at slurping up organic nutrients and vegetation is often appreciated by pond owners seeking natural alternatives to chemical algal control. Once established, a few buckets of crawfish introduced to an alga-infested pond can make the pond attractive again and inviting to swimmers (who are not crawfish-phobic).

In fact, crawfish are so voracious that non-native species introduced to some lakes and ponds can wipe out the vegetation that native fish need to live on. To prevent this, crawfish growers are usually licensed to sell only native species, and pond owners should be careful not to introduce wild varieties trapped from an "exotic" region.

Pond owners should also be aware of other potential drawbacks to stocking crawfish. Scampering across the pond bed, they can stir up sediment and create turbid water conditions. The larger varieties burrow deeply into the pond bed to reproduce and survive adverse conditions and may cause leaks. If they do become a problem, one of the best nontoxic ways to eliminate crawfish is to introduce a variety of crawfish-loving game fish, like bass or trout. If your pond already supports game fish, it may be impossible to establish a crawfish population until they are removed.

After more than 10 years of using crawfish to control algae in my own pond, I'm willing to accept a moderate increase in turbidity in exchange for weed-free water. And I've never found burrows to be a problem. I was happily surprised, however, to find that in addition to cleaning up vegetation, crawfish also get rid of leeches.

See *Biological Aquatic Plant Management.*

Crushed Stone

Various grades of crushed stone are used in and around ponds. Riprap, a large grade of broken rock, is used in inflow and outflow channels to prevent erosion; it can also be used on the backslope of pond embankments to stabilize the dam. (Riprap is a common sight along roads and highways and has an industrial look some pond owners may not like.) Crushed stone, a smaller manufactured rock, can also be used to stabilize water channels; some pond owners use it around the shoreline to prevent wave damage and to discourage burrowing by muskrats. A layer of crushed stone packed into a clay liner helps prevent drying and cracking when the clay is exposed to air. Crushed stone is also used to fill upslope drainage ditches (sometimes around perforated pipe) to prevent sedimentation. Gravel, a small pulverized rock, can be added to the area where a stream enters a pond to create a nesting area for breeding trout.

See *Clay*, *Erosion,* and *Liners.*

Dams

Technically, dams are barriers that can be made from a variety of materials—wood, steel, earth, concrete—and are most often used to impound water. An earthen embankment is a type of dam.

See *Embankment*.

Dam Safety and Liability

Pond ownership often confers responsibility for downstream damage due to pond flooding. In particular, owners of dammed ponds may be liable for damage caused by dam failure. Depending on the size of the pond and downstream assets, dam failure can have a devastating effect on people and property. The Association of State Dam Safety Officials publishes useful guidelines for pond owners concerned about dam safety.

Builders of large state or federally regulated dams are usually required to hire engineers to design the dam and conform to construction plans. During operation, owners should periodically inspect the dam for signs of flooding, seepage, leaks, or structural decay. Dam failure may be caused by poor design or construction, seepage, frost damage, flooding, burrowing animals, pipe or concrete spillway failure, and more. Depending on the severity of deterioration or flooding, the owner should implement an emergency plan (often involving dewatering), call 911 and/or the state dam safety officer, or call an engineer to assess the potential for failure and need for repair.

Contact your state dam safety officer or the Association of Dam Safety Officials (450 Old East Vine Street, Lexington, Kentucky 40507; 606 257-5140) for more information.

See *Dam*, *Embankment*, and *Liability*.

Bubblers or other aeration equipment can be used to keep part of a pond ice-free, enhance waterfowl habitat, and maintain healthy oxygen levels for fish.

Deicing

Pond owners raising fish may wish to continue feeding through the winter. In the North the ice can be kept open by operating an aeration system. The most energy-efficient deicer is a compressed-air bubbler, which can be run by electricity or (less reliably) a windpump. Long winters under ice can lead to low-dissolved-oxygen problems, especially in stocked ponds. In addition to keeping the pond open for feeding, aerators maintain healthy oxygen levels and vent toxic gases. *Caution:* Holes in the ice are dangerous and weaken surrounding ice. Locate bubblers or splashers near a dock or pier or shore, so you can feed from a solid structure, and do not skate or walk on weakened ice.

See *Aeration*.

Detention Ponds

Also known as *sediment ponds, storm water ponds,* and *retention ponds,* they're used for flood and erosion control as well as pollutant and nutrient catchments. Detention ponds are generally required by environmental agencies in connection with construction projects and developments, where builders must comply with requirements to manage storm water runoff, soil erosion, nonpoint pollution, and hazardous material spills. They are also popular with architects required to include them in developments, who soon discover that they become an aesthetic focus as well as a water management technique. Developers and architects have learned that water sells property.

A well-designed detention pond serves the practical purpose of water-quality control during construction, and upon completion adds a landscaping asset. How does it work? Runoff above the pond is usually absorbed and filtered by soil. When soil is replaced by pavement, buildings, drains, and so on, runoff and pollution increase and move faster. If directed into a detention pond, however, silt and contaminants settle to the bottom, and the cleaner discharge overflows into the downstream watershed. Result: a natural filtration system, especially when augmented by pollutant-absorbing aquatic plants. (Supplemental aeration may be required to circulate water and maintain oxygen levels.) Detention ponds may require a liner to prevent leakage and perhaps a source of supplementary water to maintain optimal levels and water quality. Water testing is done periodically.

With all elements working together, a detention pond is a valuable biological system. Several studies, however, have pointed out flaws in the catchment strategy. Excessive algal growth can be a problem due to high nutrient loads. Seasonal turnover of cold water in deep ponds brings up sediment and nutrients, which may escape downstream. During storms, agitated water may stir up sediment, resulting in an outflow of water more polluted than the inflow. In addition, ponds with low, stagnant water cycles may harbor mosquitoes, a growing concern with the outbreak of the West Nile virus.

Success of detention ponds depends on the quality of runoff flowing in and the creation of good internal dynamics. It's not wise to count on uniform success from a simple one-size-fits-all approach.

See *Sediment Pools* and *Silt Fence.*

Diaphragm

See *Anti-Seep Collars.*

Diffuser

Used in aeration systems to disperse air, or sometimes pure oxygen, into water. Air is pumped into the water through a hose and then released through holes in the diffuser, which is usually positioned on the pond or lake bottom. Diffusers can be made from metal pipe, hose, plastic, or ceramic "airstones." Ceramic diffusers are considered one of the most effective bubblers. They can be designed to release air bubbles through thousands of microscopic holes, which create a highly efficient oxygen transfer. The upward flow of bubbles also helps set up a current that intermixes different temperature layers, destratifying the water. Diffusers are very effective at introducing air into oxygen-starved lower layers of water, which aids in the decomposition of organic matter and can improve fish health. Ceramic airstones and other diffusers may require periodic cleaning to keep the holes from becoming clogging.

See *Aeration.*

Digger Ponds

Stream pools that use the energy of flowing water to dig themselves as well as help keep the basin sediment-free. Also called a *log pyramid pool digger,* the digger pond was popularized by conservation agencies as a technique for creating

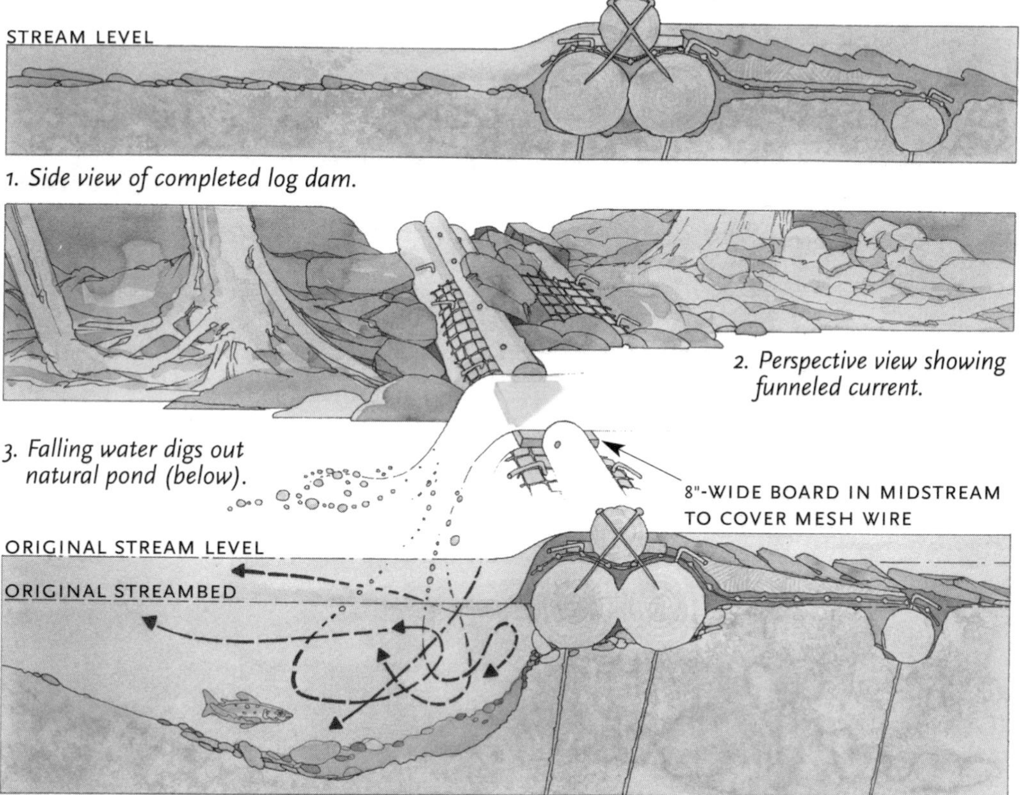

1. *Side view of completed log dam.*

2. *Perspective view showing funneled current.*

3. *Falling water digs out natural pond (below).*

fish-friendly stream pools. A dam is constructed in the waterway upstream of the pool area, and water cascading over the dam carves out a plunge pool. The digger pond is oxygen rich, which is good for fish, and the dam itself is notched in the middle, or stepped, to ensure a water flow during low-water periods. Thus the dam does not block fish from moving up- or downstream, for migration, feedings, and so forth.

The digger pond is also useful for creating stream pools to supply water for nearby ponds or hydropower. Unlike conventional stream pools that feature a dam on the downstream end to create a reservoir, and often load up with sediment, the digger pond is less likely to plug the feed pipe. Digger ponds can also be used for wading, saunas, irrigation, stock water, and more.

Dam construction should be done during low-water periods, incorporating a central notch or stepped effect that ensures continuous flow. Depending on the size of the stream, the state and/or Army Corps of Engineers may have jurisdiction over construction, and dam building may be prohibited or require a permit.

Discharge

See *Overflow*.

Diversion Ditch

See *Berm, Drainage Field,* and *Swale.*

Docks and Piers

These terms are often used interchangeably in reference to constructed platforms built along shore or projecting into the water. Docks are generally built parallel to shore, providing a location for boats to tie up, access for repairs, and so forth. Piers project out into the water, for similar purposes. Docks and piers can be good places to fish, swim, and generally enjoy waterfront access. Docks

This homemade rolling pier can be adjusted to changing water levels, and removed in winter to prevent ice damage and make room for skaters.

and piers can be built on rigid supports (stone, concrete, wooden piers), floats, or a combination of both. Using a flotation system gives the structure versatility. A floating system adapts to changing water levels and can be designed to be brought up on shore during the winter to prevent ice damage. Rigid structures are generally used where stability is preferred (pedestrian traffic, boat hoists, commercial use, and the like). One clever pond pier design combines mobility and rigidity by incorporating large wheels at the far end, so the pier can be rolled in and out of the water and adjusted for water level. Water-level flexibility (a floating or rolling dock) is especially useful in ponds with variable water levels.

Because wood exposed to the weather is vulnerable to decay, docks and piers are sometimes constructed using chemically treated lumber. Many of these chemicals, especially arsenic, can be harmful to aquatic life, as well as the builder and those who use the structure. Using chemically treated lumber may be against the law, depending on the location. Naturally decay-resistant lumber such as cedar, hemlock, or recycled plastic.

Domestic Water Supply Pond

In some rural areas of the United States and Canada, poor soil and inadequate groundwater will not support reliable wells, and ponds can be set up to supply domestic water. Getting good drinking water from a pond should start with the cleanest water possible. The watershed feeding the pond should be free of farm animals, septic system runoff, fertilizers and pesticides, and any other obvious contamination. Engineers with the USDA suggest that it's best if the pond's entire watershed is controlled by the pond owner, with no roads crossing the watershed because of the pollution potential. A protective buffer of dense grass 100 feet or more wide should surround the pond. If you plan to use an existing pond, test the water before installing the system. Evaporation can be minimized with a small surface area and deep volume design—at least 8 feet deep, and perhaps deeper in the North to ensure that ice doesn't interfere with the intake system. Pond size will depend on the volume of inflow and size of the watershed. In areas where the pond will fill only once in spring, it should be at least 200,000 gallons; bigger if watershed and spring flows are minimal. To keep animals out, the pond should be protected by a fence at least 100 feet from the shoreline. Steep sides will reduce aquatic vegetation, and aquatic plants should not be introduced. Swimming should be prohibited. Algae may be controlled by biological predators such as crawfish, zooplankton, and grass carp. If chemical controls are needed, consult your health department.

A float-suspended intake anchored offshore is recommended for removing water. Inside the house, a pump and purification system treats the water. Engineers recommend a carbon filter and/or chlorinator or iodizer to purify the water. Ultraviolet light systems can also purify water without the use of chemicals. The water should be tested periodically for bacteria and other contaminants.

Dowsing

Skill, superstition, or just plain magic? Whatever you think of dowsing, the bottom line for many people is: it works.

The ability to locate subterranean water with a forked wooden stick or other "divining" tool, including metal and plastic rods and pendular bobs on the end of a string. Dowsing, also known as *water witching* and *divining,* reputedly can be used to find just about anything the dowser is looking for, including lost objects, missing children, and buried treasure. Despite plenty of debunkers, dowsing for water is a rural folk skill with a successful history dating back hundreds of years, and it is still used by some pond builders to help locate sites and find wells and springs.

Although there is no conclusive scientific theory that explains how dowsing works, studies of successful dowsers suggest it may be connected to their sensitivity to changes in electromagnetic fields associated with subterranean water. Still, this doesn't explain how some dowsers can find water or other objects on a map, far from the area in question.

The traditional method for dowsing water involves holding a forked stick, palms down, and walking the land until the stick pulls down, pointing out where the water lies. Depending how hard the stick pulls, successful dowsers are often able to determine the depth of the water below ground and the volume of flow.

Some advanced water witches are able to “ask” their sticks about depth, capacity, and quality, and receive answering tugs.

Governmental agencies and well drillers often debunk the dowsing phenomenon, but I’ve seen successful wells and ponds located by dowsing. My household water comes from a gravity-feed spring discovered by a dowser using a forked stick he cut from a branch just minutes before he found the water. Pond leaks, often notoriously difficult to pinpoint, can also be tracked down by a good dowser.

For further information, check out Christopher Bird’s classic book on dowsing, *The Divining Hand* (Whitford Press); and the American Dowser’s Society, P.O. Box 24, Danville, VT 05828, 802-684-3417.

Dragline

An excavating crane with a digging bucket attached by cables to a long boom and operated by being dropped on the digging surface and dragged back toward the machine by cable. Draglines are often used to dig excavated ponds in saturated soil and for pond

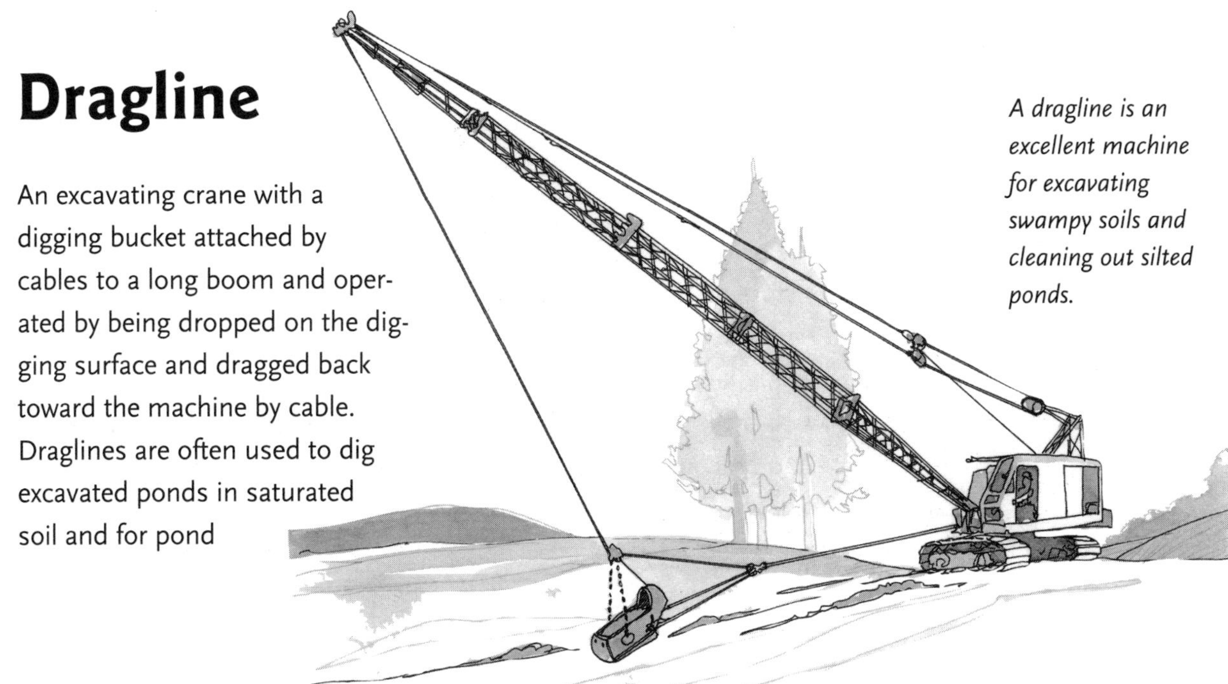

A dragline is an excellent machine for excavating swampy soils and cleaning out silted ponds.

cleanouts. Because of the long reach of the boom, draglines can dig large ponds from a firm shoreline position. Draglines sometimes work on a portable mat, which the operator can position in wet areas to create a stable working platform. Dragline pond excavation tends to take more working hours per cubic foot of volume created than a bulldozer and/or excavator building an embankment pond. Draglines should not be expected to perform well at compacting dams or finish grading.

Dragonflies

See *Biological Insect Pest Control.*

Drain

A pipe used to lower a pond's water level, or drain the pond completely. Drains are usually installed in embankment ponds on sloping terrain, because on flat terrain you can't run the pipe to daylight. Ideally installed deep enough in the pond to be able to drain most water, the intake should be sited where it will not be covered with accumulating sediment. Drains can be installed by themselves or connected to drop-inlet spillway pipes. Either way, the pipe through the dam should be carefully compacted and fitted with anti-seep collars to prevent leakage around the outside of the pipe.

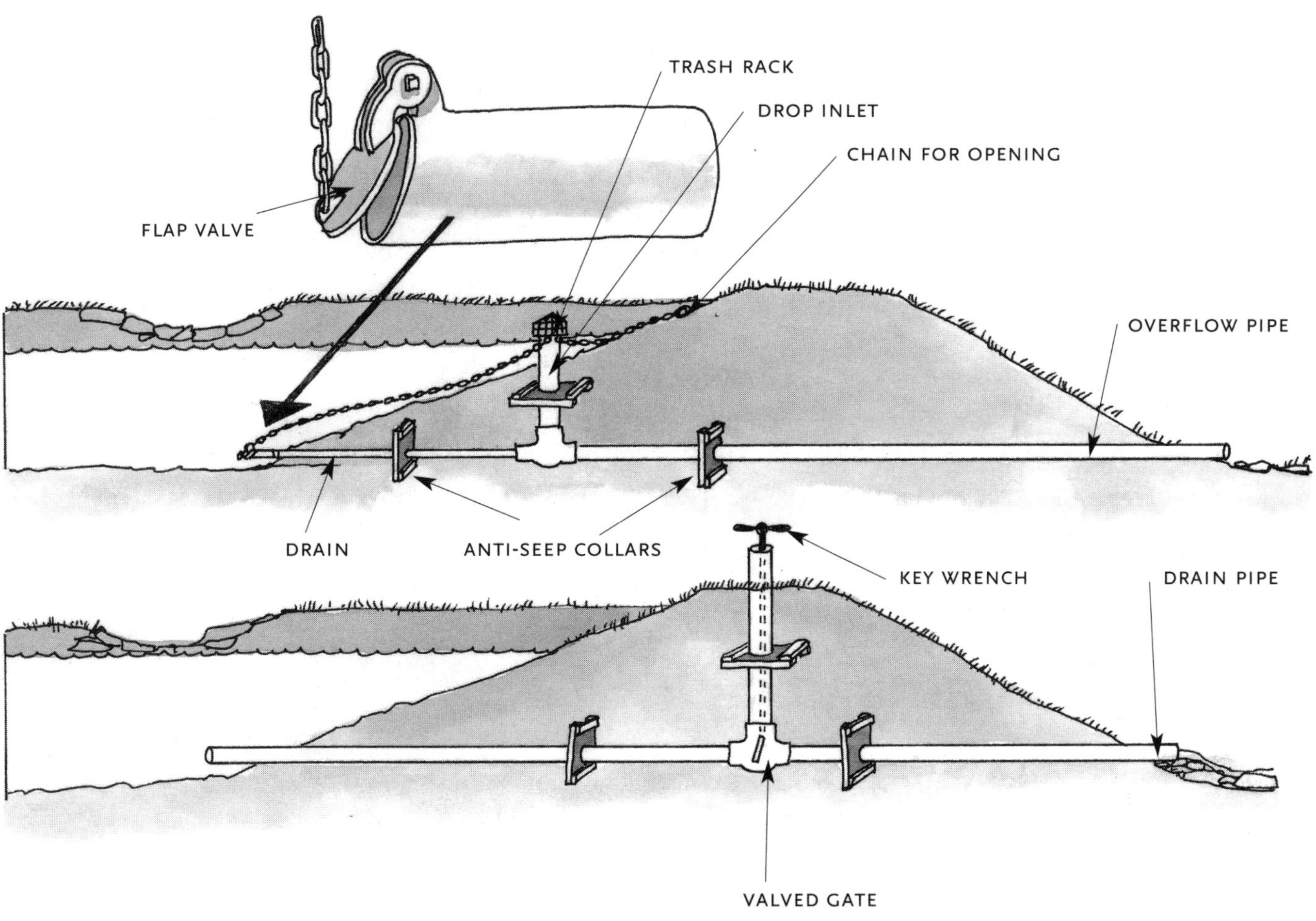

Drains are used by pond owners to simplify water releases for repairs, drawdowns, and fish harvests. They can be built into drop inlet systems with flap gates (top) or as independent units with variable flow valves.

Control valves for drains are usually a flapper valve on the intake end of the pipe or a shut-off valve in the pipe itself. Flapper valves are often opened by pulling a rope or chain attached to the valve; shut-off valves are usually controlled by an iron bar lowered through an access pipe in the dam. Often flapper valves are used to completely drain a pond because once open they may be difficult to close again tightly, until the pond is dry. Shut-off valves allow for more on–off control, and can be used for partial drawdowns to control shoreline vegetation, pier or beach work, fish harvests, and so on. Draining all the water may be necessary for cleanouts, repairs, and installing liners or sealants. Over the years, drains with flapper valves tend to get buried under sediment. They can sometimes be banged open from the outside with a long pipe. I heard about one character who used a shotgun, but considering the potential for ricochet, I wouldn't recommend it.

See *T-Riser.*

Drainage Field

The area around a pond may be highly saturated, causing erosion or unmanageably wet soils. Ditches, sometimes combined with drainage piping, can be used to control runoff and groundwater flow. Depending on whether the water is needed for the pond or not, a ditch or swale can be dug to deflect the water away from the pond, or into it. Ditches that dry out terrain and run water into a pond usually benefit from being combined with crushed stone and pipe (perforated or solid, sometimes both), covered with soil, and seeded. This has the advantage of drying out wet terrain, bringing water into the pond, and preventing erosion. Pipes are sometimes fitted with vertical vents, which prevent air locking and allow the pipe to be flushed of sediment, if needed.

See *Watershed.*

Drawdown

The lowering of pond water, or complete dewatering, for repairs, dredging, weed control, or fish or other crop harvests. A partial drawdown of several feet is a popular technique for control of unwanted shoreline vegetation and algae. Nuisance weeds can be manually removed when the water level is lowered, and the drying effects of sun and air help kill submergent vegetation. In the North a drawdown that extends into winter months allows frost to penetrate the soil and kill pond weeds. Care should be taken not to expose piping to possible frost damage or clay liners to dehydration, cracking, and leaks.

The benefits of a deliberate drawdown can sometimes be duplicated during droughty conditions, when pond water levels drop naturally, and weeds can be removed manually and shore areas raked and cleaned. If possible, water inflows should be cut off during natural or deliberate drawdowns.

Drawdowns can be accomplished using drainpipes built into the pond structure. If there are no drains in a pond, pumping or siphoning will be necessary.

Aquatic weeds can be controlled by dropping the pond water level to dry out roots and simplify manual cleanup.

Water should be released gradually to prevent downstream erosion. Drainpipes are usually about 4 inches in diameter, even when coupled to larger drop inlets, to prevent downstream erosion during a drawdown or complete dewatering. Some pond owners find that where the downstream grade is steep enough, siphoning with a flexible 4-inch plastic pipe, such as elephant trunk, allows them also to suck up accumulated sediment during the drawdown. A trash pump could accomplish the same objective.

Drawdowns were originally used by farmers and aquaculturists tending multiple ponds to harvest a crop and let the pond lie fallow for a time, allowing the antiseptic effects of sun and air to rejuvenate the basin. Exposed to the air, anaerobic sediments decomposed, parasites died, and aquatic vegetation could be cleaned up and grass crops grown in the rich pond soil. Additionally, volunteer plants or cultivated crops produced seeds that attracted waterfowl for hunting when the pond was refilled. Pond rotation also allowed fish farmers to raise and harvest fish of one size or species in each pond, without mixing fry and mature grades.

The negative side of the drawdown is the loss of cultivated and natural life. Many pond owners who plan drawdowns as part of a cleanup regime are concerned about losing fish, frogs, and other critters. Prior to a complete drawdown, fish should be caught out, or seined and transferred (unless, of course, they're being intentionally eliminated). I also recommend gradual drawdowns to allow pond critters to find another habitat. Keep in mind that even a partial drawdown may stress fish enough to kill them.

See *Moist-Soil Management.*

Dredging

The excavation of native material or sediment in the process of either digging or cleaning out a pond (or a larger body of water). Equipment for dredging includes floating dredges, draglines, and excavators. Dredging usually involves the removal of saturated material, which is a slower process than digging or dozing drier earth, and requires removal or creative use of large amounts of fill.

See *Cleanout, Dragline, Excavation,* and *Excavator.*

Drip Irrigation

A farm and garden watering system that uses perforated hoses on the surface or buried between the rows. The source can be household water or an external source. Ponds are often used as a water source for farm and garden irrigation. The pump can be powered by electricity, gas, a hydraulic ram, or wind. Gardeners often locate a garden downhill from a pond to take advantage of gravity flow.

See *Irrigation Ponds.*

Drop Inlet

A vertical overflow structure (pipe, box, or the like) connected to the main section of a spillway system.

See *T-Riser.*

Drought

Depending on its severity, a drought can beat a pond, or a pond can beat a drought. If pond water levels drop significantly, fish may die because of high temperatures and low dissolved oxygen levels. Warm, stagnant water often triggers algal blooms which further degrade water quality. Supplementary water, aeration, and even ice may be used as remedies to rally water quality.

Even a pond half full of water may be able to irrigate a garden and crops, provide water for animals, and back up diminished household water, if not for drinking, but for washing dishes, flushing, and so forth (as long as drawdowns don't endanger fish). The pond may continue to have the potential to fight fires, which are likely to be a concurrent risk. Many pond owners take advantage of low water periods to do that sediment cleanout they've been putting off. Is your pond half-full or half-empty?

See *Aeration, Cleanout, Domestic Water Supply Pond, Dry Hydrant, Firefighting Ponds, Irrigation Ponds, Leaks, Liners, Sealants, Stagnant Water, Well,* and *Windpumps.*

Fire protection is one of the traditional benefits of a pond. A dry hydrant ensures quick access and an ice-free flow in cold climates.

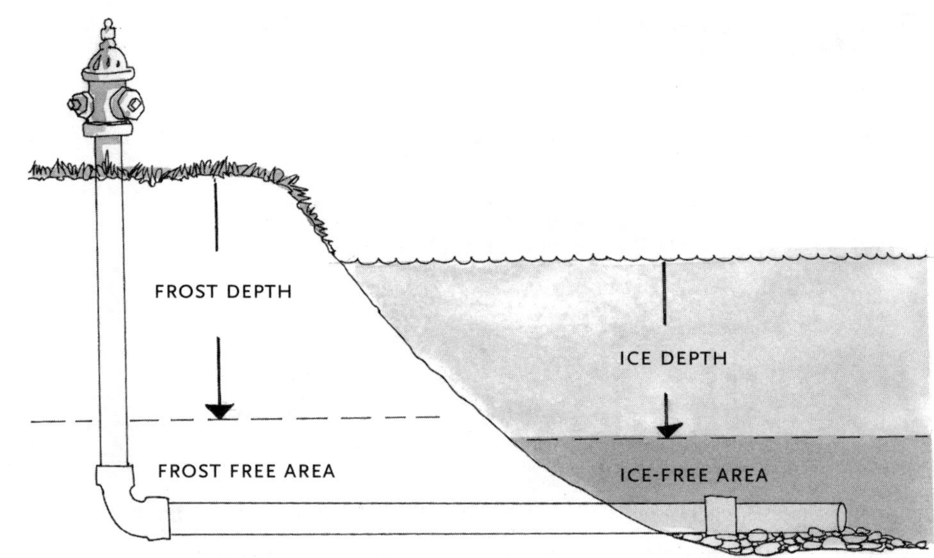

Dry Hydrant

Similar in appearance to the municipal fire hydrants seen along streets, except that it's set up near a pond. And instead of being connected to a pressurized city water system, a dry hydrant is plumbed to an intake in the pond. In case of fire, a pumper truck hooks up to the dry hydrant and draws out water to fight the blaze. Dry hydrants have two big advantages over drawing water directly from a pond: they can be set up in an area easily accessible to a fire truck, and with an intake deep underwater, they avoid ice problems in winter. Dry hydrants should be installed so that the intake is deep enough to prevent freezing during the winter (the vertical hydrant itself is "dry" until pumping begins) and high enough off the pond bed to prevent clogging by sediment. The intake is usually screened to prevent damage to the hydrant and pump from mud and debris. Hydrants can also be used for irrigation, agricultural spraying, livestock watering, and other water requirements.

See *firefighting Ponds.*

Ducks

Similar to geese in their potential to be raised domestically for profit or pleasure, as well as wild varieties being attracted by planting cover and food crops and manipulating water levels. The wild varieties are not likely to cause the kinds of pest problems that geese can. Also used by some pond managers for alga control.

See *Biological Aquatic Plant Management, Moist-Soil Management, and Waterfowl.*

Dugout

There are two types of ponds: embankment (or dammed) and dugout (excavated). Dugouts are just that—dug out of the ground in relatively flat terrain, with no need for a dam. Construction is pretty straightforward. For every bucket

Dugout (excavated) ponds are built on flat terrain and may need to be protected against seasonal flooding.

of earth removed, you get a bucket of water. Dugouts are especially popular in the Midwest as well as the plains states and provinces, where the land is flat and farms need water for livestock and irrigation.

Dugouts usually require a uniformly clay-rich soil to hold water, especially if excavation precludes construction of a clay liner. Dugouts are often supplied by groundwater and/or runoff. If the main source is groundwater, the permanent water table should be close to ground level. Runoff sources should be monitored to prevent contamination by agricultural chemicals or other pollution. Overflow is usually channeled through an earth-cut spillway back into natural drainageways. The spillway should be reinforced against erosion. Sometimes a protective berm or terrace is built around the pond to prevent flooding. This can be an effective way to use some of the material excavated from the pond. Larger earthen mounds can also be used as "privacy mounds," windbreaks, or snow fences; otherwise the excavated material can be spread around. Dugouts are often excavated in rectangular shape for ease of construction and deeper than embankment ponds to reduce evaporation.

Conservationists have built and managed dugouts along migratory waterfowl flyways to create refuge and feeding areas for ducks, geese, and other birds. These ponds have been significant in the recovery of dwindling waterfowl populations.

See *Excavation*.

Dye

There are several types of dyes that can be used in ponds. Most familiar are the blue dyes used to stop algal and plant growth. By preventing sunlight from penetrating the water, these dyes cut off photosynthesis and kill aquatic vegetation. To be effective, however, dyes must be used in the right aquatic conditions, and application recommendations must be followed. In fact, only a few commercially available dyes have met EPA pesticide qualifications. To cut off beneficial sunlight wavelengths, the dye has to be the right color or it won't work.

Ponds respond best to dye treatment when there is no overflow. Any significant water exchange is going to cause dilution of the dye, making it less effective. Overflowing dye can also pollute downstream waters. Dyes may be regulated by local and state government; in some states, you need a permit or license to use an aquatic dye.

It's important to follow the manufacturer's dilution recommendation. Several liquid dyes require about a gallon of concentrate per 1 million gallons of water, or roughly a 1-acre pond 4 feet deep. Even so-called organic dyes should be carefully applied. In dilution, they will not cause staining, but protective gloves and eyewear should be worn when applying the concentrate. To be effective, the dye should make it impossible to see your fish, although plant growth may be stopped only below 2 or 3 feet.

Cutting off photosynthesis does have a potential negative effect. By preventing plant growth, you also cut off oxygen production, and in some ponds with low dissolved oxygen, the introduction of a dye can cause a fish-kill. Using dye combined with aeration may overcome this. Cutting off plant growth may also eliminate food for fish and wildlife. Some people object to the artificial color, although there are those who find it attractive.

Dyes are not only used as algaecides. They can also be mixed with chemicals to indicate actual dispersal, and are sometimes used to detect leaks. Fluorescent-tinted dyes are most effective at revealing leaks surfacing outside the pond; one pond builder I know pours dairy cream in the water to detect leaks inside the pond.

See *Alga* and *Leaks.*

Electrofishing

A technique used by fish and wildlife departments to sample the fish populations in sport-fishing ponds and lakes. Using specially outfitted boats and working in shallow shore areas, personnel electrify the water around the boat. fish are temporarily stunned, netted into a boat well, measured and counted, and the majority are released alive. Mortality is low. By sampling a lake's fish, biologists can create a profile of the various species and determine the desirability of the existing population. Depending on the results, adjustments may be made (more bass or trout needed, for example) to create a healthy sport-fishing mix. Electroshocking is generally restricted to public waters and not used in private ponds. Fish populations can also be determined by seining.

See *Seines*.

Elephant Trunk

Flexible corrugated plastic pipe with versatile applications around ponds. It's used for water capture and diversion, as a siphon to draw down or empty a pond, and even as a silt vacuum during siphoning. Perforated elephant trunk can be used underground for drainage. T's and elbows are available.

Elodea *(Elodea canadensis)*

Also called waterweed or Canadian pondweed, Elodea is a good oxygen producer in water gardens but invasive in recreational ponds.

A submerged aquatic plant favored by water gardeners as oxygenator and biofilter. It provides food for some species of waterfowl and shelter for insects valuable as fish food. Like many aquatic plants that support wildlife, elodea may be invasive and thus a problem if introduced in recreational ponds.

See *Biological Plant Management* and *Invasive Exotic Plants.*

Embankment

A constructed earthen barrier used to impound water, most often built on the downstream side of a sloping site. Embankments, or dams, are commonly found in agricultural and recreational ponds, where the cost of a concrete dam would be prohibitive. They can be built across a draw to impound a stream, or more often on sloping terrain—combined with an excavated pond basin—to hold streams, springs, and watershed runoff. Material from the excavated basin is often used to build the embankment.

The foundation under a dam must be stable enough to support the embankment and resist seepage. Porous embankment materials may provide good support without satisfactory water retention, and require a sealant. High-clay-content soils hold water but may not provide support for very large dams; the best foundation material is a mixture of coarse- and fine-textured soils. Dams can also be built on rock, which should not be fractured or liable to leakage.

The ideal fill material for the dam will come from the pond site itself; importing material is expensive. The best dam material should contain about 20 percent clay (see *Test Pits*). Most dams, especially those using coarse-textured soils,

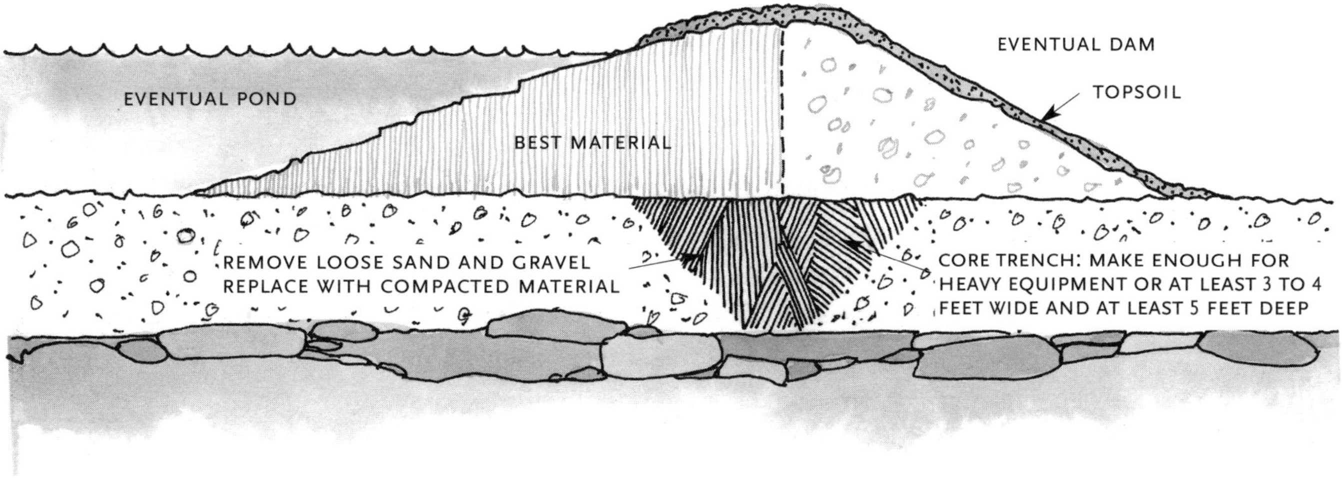

EVENTUAL DAM
TOPSOIL
EVENTUAL POND
BEST MATERIAL
REMOVE LOOSE SAND AND GRAVEL
REPLACE WITH COMPACTED MATERIAL
CORE TRENCH: MAKE ENOUGH FOR
HEAVY EQUIPMENT OR AT LEAST 3 TO 4
FEET WIDE AND AT LEAST 5 FEET DEEP

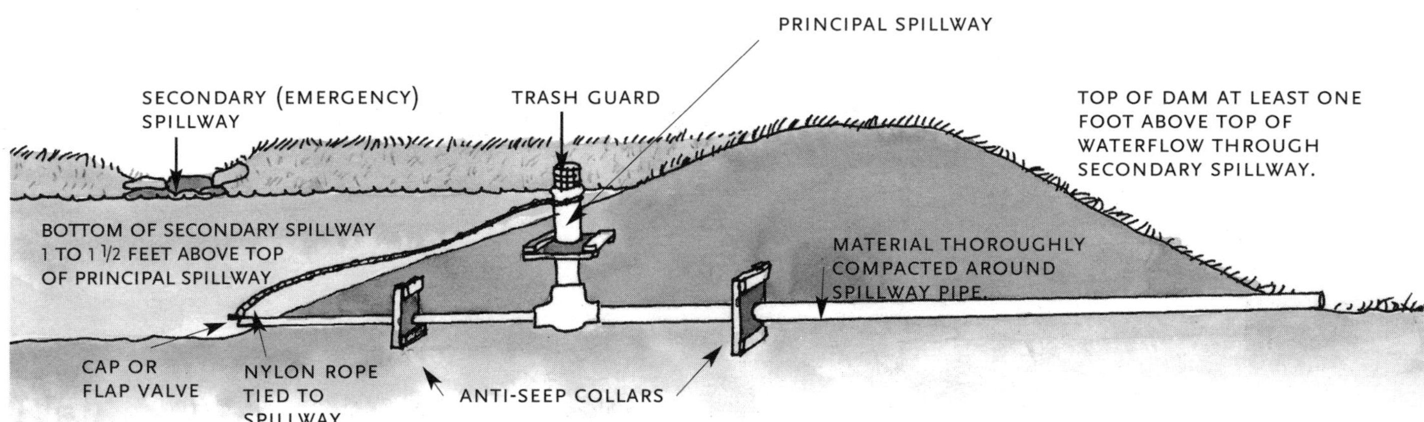

Earthen dam used to impound water on sloping terrain. Embankments require good soil, a core trench, thorough compaction, correct slopes, sufficient freeboard, and a correctly sized spillway (with anti-seep collars if pipe is used).

incorporate a cutoff core of impervious material at the base and/or a layer of clay on the upstream side. During construction of the dam, the best fill should be used on the upstream side. Embankments should be built in layers approximately 1 foot thick and compacted.

The size of the dam will depend on height and foundation material. The USDA suggests a minimum top width of 6 feet for dams less than 10 feet high, increasing as the elevation rises. Side slopes should be roughly 3 to 1. Dams built on less stable soils should incorporate flatter slopes to better distribute the weight. No organic matter, such as tree stumps, should be buried in the dam, where they can decompose and lead to slumping and leaks.

Embankments must be built with enough freeboard above the pond water level, as well as sufficient spillway systems, to prevent flooding during storms and high-runoff periods. Tree plantings are discouraged in dams because of the potential for root damage to the structure. Fertilizer is also discouraged, to prevent nutrient loading in the pond. Embankments are usually curved, perhaps irregularly, to give the pond a natural look, and the top of a dam often makes a good area for recreation and perhaps an outbuilding.

See *Core Trench.*

Emergency Spillway

Designing a primary spillway to discharge peak runoff from the most intense rainstorm imaginable is impractical. Therefore, an earth-cut emergency spillway is usually installed to convey surface runoff that may exceed the capacity of the main spillway. Embankment ponds with pipe overflow spillways are most likely to require emergency spillways. Emergency spillways are usually designed according to the size of the pond drainage area, height of the dam, and USDA storm frequency charts. Without an emergency spillway, excess overflow could breach the dam, causing possible damage to the embankment and downstream flooding. Excavated ponds can also benefit from emergency spillways.

See *Watershed.*

Erosion

Weathering and chemical processes that wear down rocks and soil particles and transport eroded material downhill. Ponds can be particularly vulnerable to erosion occurring in the watershed above the pond, in the structure itself, and below the pond. Erosion in the watershed and feeder streams can lead to silt and sediment accumulation in the pond. This can happen slowly over time, or rapidly in watersheds affected by agriculture, logging, development, or harsh weather. Erosion is also likely to be a problem in newly constructed ponds if

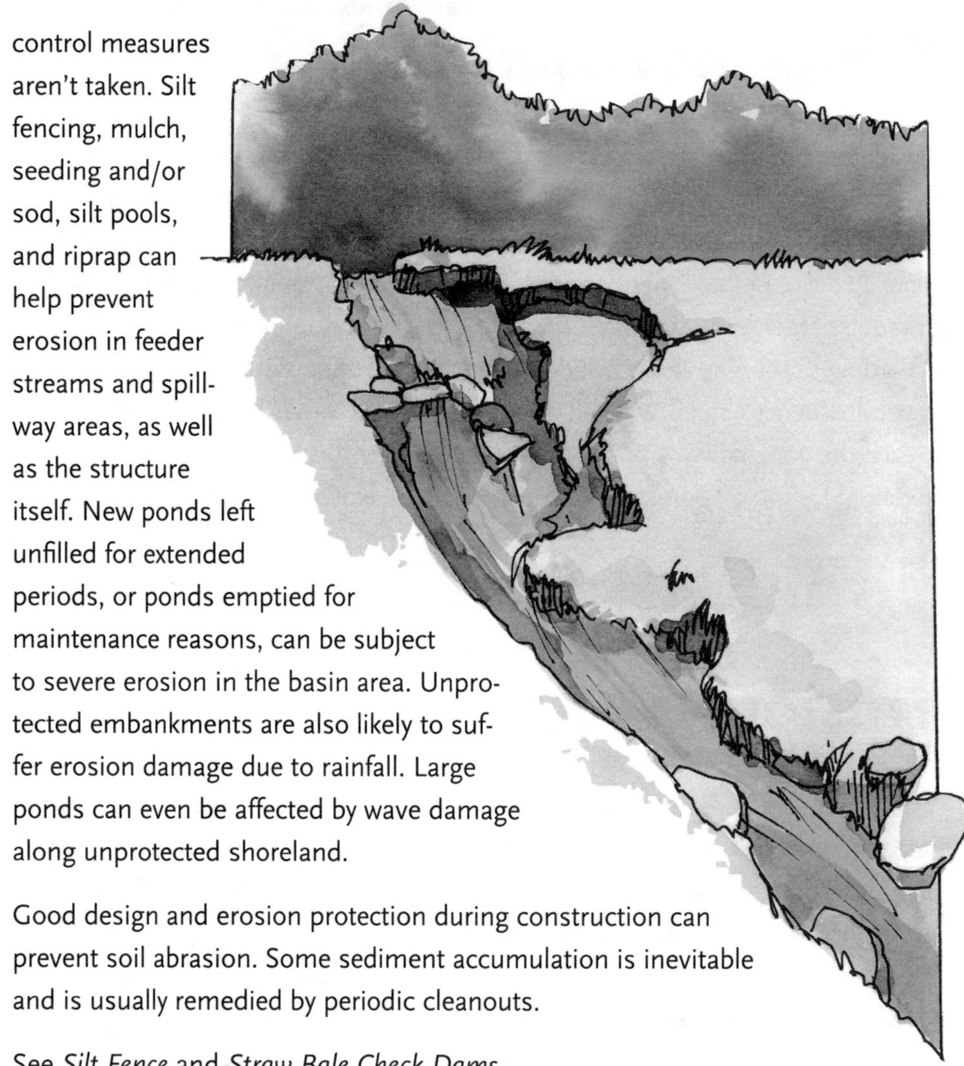

Faulty construction or extreme weather can lead to erosion severe enough to destroy a pond.

control measures aren't taken. Silt fencing, mulch, seeding and/or sod, silt pools, and riprap can help prevent erosion in feeder streams and spillway areas, as well as the structure itself. New ponds left unfilled for extended periods, or ponds emptied for maintenance reasons, can be subject to severe erosion in the basin area. Unprotected embankments are also likely to suffer erosion damage due to rainfall. Large ponds can even be affected by wave damage along unprotected shoreland.

Good design and erosion protection during construction can prevent soil abrasion. Some sediment accumulation is inevitable and is usually remedied by periodic cleanouts.

See *Silt Fence* and *Straw Bale Check Dams.*

Eurasian Water Milfoil
(Myriophyllum spicatum L)

This rapidly spreading non-native aquatic plant is spoiling lakes and ponds across the country.

An invasive exotic aquatic plant that infests rivers, lakes, and ponds in the continental United States. Once established, Eurasian water milfoil outcompetes native plants and forms thick mats that interfere with recreation and fish spawning. Milfoil grows along shorelines and in water up to 30 feet deep. Native to Europe and Asia, it was brought to North America as an aquarium plant, and spread accidentally. It may also have been introduced by ships dumping ballast water.

Once established, milfoil is almost impossible to eradicate. Control measures to limit its spread include manual removal, mechanical harvesters, bottom barriers, chemicals, and biological controls such as grass carp and aquatic weevils. Smaller bodies of water can sometimes be managed with dredging and drawdowns. The best milfoil preventive is to stop it from entering a body of water to begin with. Boats, trailers, and other aquatic equipment should be inspected before entering an uncontaminated area.

See *Biological Aquatic Plant Management* and *Invasive Exotic Plants.*

Eutrophication

A natural process in ponds and lakes that leads to increasing fertility and biological production levels and decreasing basin volume. Eutrophication is usually associated with an undesired reduction in dissolved oxygen levels and an increase in algae and turbidity. It's caused by loading of silt, organic and nonorganic matter, and nutrients. Once the process begins, increases in shallow areas and aquatic plant growth usually accelerate, as decaying vegetation feeds the process. Eventually, if not curtailed, eutrophication will lead to the "death" of a pond and the birth of a swamp or wetland.

See *Aeration, Biological Aquatic Plant Management,* and *Cleanout.*

Excavation

The process of digging the fill out of a pond site. In the case of an excavated-only pond, when the digging is complete, so is the pond. Sometimes excavation is done in tandem with preparation and construction of a pond embankment, often using material from the excavation to build the dam.

See *Cleanout, Dragline, Dredging, Dugout,* and *Excavator.*

Excavator

A mechanical digger with a hinged bucket attached to a long hydraulic arm, used for excavating or moving soil, gravel, clay, sand, and so forth. Often mounted on tracks and able to work in wet conditions, excavators make good pond-building and cleanout machines, digging quickly and accurately. Excavators are often teamed up with a bulldozer for construction of embankment ponds.

A variety of bucket designs makes it possible for a pond builder to use an excavator for stonework as well as digging.

Fertilizer

Enrichment of fish ponds is a well-proven, traditional technique used by some growers to enhance warm-water crops such as carp, catfish, tilapia, and so on. Commercial fertilizer, manure, or sewage can be used to stimulate photoplankton, which in turn nourishes the fish. Agricultural limestone can also be used to raise pH, which in turn creates more fertile waters. Fertilization has a potential downside, however:

stimulation of excessive aquatic growth can lead to pond eutrophication, oxygen loss, and fish mortality. Some aquaculture professionals sternly warn against fertilizing recreational fish ponds because of these liabilities. Today, most professional aquaculturists depend on specially formulated feeds to grow fish. (In fact, fish waste acts as a fertilizer itself, supplying needed nutrients.) Polyculture systems that combine agriculture and aquaculture take advantage of naturally occurring manure to enrich fish crops—ducks raised in a fish pond, for example. Natural pond fertilization can be especially effective in developing countries and on small farms because of low capital costs. Cold-water fish such as trout are not raised in fertilized water.

See *Polyculture.*

Filters

Water filtration is more often a requirement of small fish and garden pools than large ponds. For small pools, water is usually recirculated by pump through biological or mechanical filters. Larger earth ponds are not likely to require filtration because fresh water is naturally introduced to the system, and biological systems support decomposition of organic nutrients and oxygen production. Some larger ponds with water-quality problems can benefit from filtration. Public recreational ponds may use sand filters to clean inflow streams or to purify mechanically recirculated water.

Newly constructed ponds often require sediment filters to prevent silt from entering or leaving the site. Geotextile fabrics are used to screen inflow and outflow channels disturbed by excavation and subject to erosion. Filter fabrics can also prevent turbid ponds from silting downstream waters. Filter fabrics are installed across inflow and outflow channels and usually staked to create a "silt fence." Hay bales can also be effective at reducing sediment flow.

See *Domestic Water Supply Pond, Straw Bale Check Dams, Sand Filters* and *Silt Fence.*

Firefighting Ponds

One of the great benefits of a pond is its firefighting potential. Farmers and other residents of rural areas have long relied on ponds for a larger supply of water than a fire truck can carry or to supply firefighting equipment of their own. As more people move into rural areas, they may live far from a fire department (usually volunteer and modestly equipped) and appreciate that a pond supplies more water than a tanker. Rural municipalities often require that developers agree to construct fire ponds before granting a building permit. Insurance companies may give discounts to rural property owners with ponds, usually contingent on how far they live from the nearest fire department.

A pond alone isn't the best guarantee of fire safety, however, especially in winter. By installing a dry hydrant, a pond owner creates a quick hook-up system for a pumper truck, connected to an ice- and sediment-free water supply. The hydrant access should be easily open to a fire truck and plowed in winter. Rural fire departments may offer low-cost parts to a property owner installing a hydrant, and townships may give pond owners a tax break in exchange for installing a hydrant that's available to the fire department in emergencies and/or as a water source. Some states have programs that fund hydrant installation in rural areas.

See *Dry Hydrant.*

Fish Cover

Fish like hanging out near solid structures, such as stumps and rocks, for shade, nesting, protection from predators, and finding food. Constructed ponds, however, are usually built with smooth, well-compacted basins to minimize leakage and enhance swimming. If fish are stocked, they'll appreciate some irregularity on the pond bed. *Attractor, habitat,* and *structure* are some of the terms used to describe a variety of objects that can be added to improve the fish environment. Pond builders often finish off a project by building up a fish castle of large rocks in the basin. Sometimes old tires are chained together, attached to a cinder block, and dropped in the water. Aquaculture suppliers also offer prefabricated fish attractors, which have the advantage of being lightweight enough to haul out of the way for seining operations. Fish attractors should not be installed in the deepest part of the pond, to avoid problems with low oxygen levels in summer.

Fish Feeders

Many ponds will sustain a growing crop of fish naturally, depending on the species being raised, amount of forage fish, fertility, and so forth. To ensure fish health and growth, however, especially in commercial applications, pond owners often supply fish feed. In addition to manual feeding, feed can be dispensed mechanically on a continuous or intermittently timed belt feeder. Some belt feeders are spring powered and require no electricity. Various electrically powered automatic feeders are also available. Fish can also be fed using bug zappers, which attract insects to a night-light and then knock them into the water using a spinning wire or electric charge. There is some controversy regarding these zappers because of the loss of potentially beneficial insects (dragonflies, for example, which consume mosquito larvae). Demand feeders triggered by the fish themselves are also available.

Fish feeders are designed for scheduled or demand feeding.

Fish-Kill

Few sights are more distressing for the pond owner than a large crop of fish going belly-up. Fish do die of "natural" causes (old age, predation, disease), but premature mortality of small or large numbers of fish can also occur, often due to factors relating to oxygen starvation. Fish-kills are most likely to occur in summer and winter. In summer, die-offs are usually brought on by the higher metabolic rates of fish in warm water, when the greater levels of dissolved oxygen that they require are not available. This often occurs during prolonged hot and overcast weather, when lack of sunlight reduces photosynthetic oxygen production. Certain fish species react differently to high temperatures. Trout are not happy when temperatures rise much above 70 degrees F; bullheads are more heat hardy. Decaying algae and aquatic vegetation can add to lethal conditions by consuming oxygen during decomposition. Winter fish-kills often occur in northern ponds when ice and snow cut off sunlight, creating low photosynthesis. Summer and winter die-offs may be triggered by a larger fish population than a pond can sustain without supplementary oxygen.

Early signs of a kill may be fish rising to the surface seeking more thoroughly oxygenated water, and then increasing numbers going belly-up. Immediate aeration of the water may avert a fish-kill; in summer, cooling off water (ice, fresh water) may also help. In winter, clearing snow from ice-covered ponds can increase oxygen production. Northern fish growers also use aerators to maintain open water and healthy dissolved oxygen levels.

See *Aeration*.

Fish Ponds

Almost any pond can be a fish pond, considering that fish of some kind are likely to make their way to a pond whether intentionally introduced or arriving by stream, bird's foot, or neighborly donation. Still, ponds intended for fish cultivation should incorporate some basic design and water-quality elements, which will vary depending on the fish species and the amount being raised.

Fish ponds can be roughly divided into two groups: warm-water and cold-water habitats. Warm-water ponds are used to raise carp, catfish, bass, sunfish, tilapia, and the like. Cold-water ponds are home to various species of trout and perhaps other cold-water fish such as pike and muskie.

Warm-water ponds are generally shallower and more nutrient rich than cold-water ponds. Requirements for inflows of fresh water and dissolved oxygen are not as high. These ponds should be deep enough not to freeze the crop in winter, and may require aeration devices to keep part of the ice open and add oxygen. Supplemental feed or fertilization may have to be supplied. Protective cover such as rafts, piers, and dead timber and stumps, from predatory birds may also be necessary. Protective nets are also used when necessary. Watershed quality should be maintained to avoid runoff and inflows from contaminated or eroded land, which would create unhealthy water conditions. If fish are being raised for harvest by seine, there should be areas shallow enough to allow successful netting. Drains or other means of water-level drawdown may be required to facilitate harvests, cleanouts, repairs, and the like. Means for water testing should be available, especially for basic conditions such as pH, temperature, and dissolved oxygen.

Cold-water ponds for trout and other northern species require different water conditions and structural features. Trout are not going to grow well (or survive) in temperatures exceeding 65 to 70 degrees F. Because these ponds are likely to be located in northern or high-altitude regions, they should be deep enough to provide a sustainable habitat below the ice cover, which may be several feet thick. Where large crops are being raised, cold-weather aeration may be needed to prevent oxygen starvation. In fact, trout require higher dissolved oxygen year-round, making four-season aeration a necessity for large crops. Trout ponds usually feature a constant exchange of fresh water, from springs, stream, or well. Stones are often used to create fish habitat in the deepest part of the pond, for shade and protection from predators. Small crops of trout often can grow on food native to the pond (insects, crustaceans, minnows) but usually require supplemental feed to put on much weight. They are not generally raised with other fish species.

Cold-water fish ponds do share some features with warm-water habitats: submerged cover, predator protection, watershed maintenance, and water-quality monitoring. Both cold- and warm-water species can be segregated and protected in cages, although this technique requires the use of supplemental feed.

See *Bird Damage Control, Cage Culture, Fish Cover,* and *Fish Kill.*

Fish Pools

See *Water Gardens.*

Fish Removal

Fish populations may reach undesirable levels or ratios, resulting in turbid water, decreased populations of game fish, overcrowding, nutrient loading, and other unwanted effects. In game fish ponds, these problems are often due to failure to maintain a proper ratio of game and forage fish. Undesirable species levels may also be caused by mistaken or unauthorized stocking (someone drops a goldfish in your pond, your brother-in-law needs a place for his koi during a drought; pretty soon your pond is overrun and the water thick with suspended sediment particles). If wild fish get into the pond from a feeder stream, the problem may be impossible to fix without diverting the stream or setting up a filtered feed pipe.

There are several ways to deal with unwanted fish, depending on your objectives. If the plan is to keep the pond stocked with game fish, it may be possible to restore the balance of game and forage fish by stocking more predatory fish. For example, if sunfish or bluegills have overwhelmed bass, stocking more bass to feed on the forage fish may restore the equilibrium (about 10 to 1 forage fish to bass). Another way to increase game fish is to enhance their habitat. Creating fish rubble habitat for walleyes has proven effective, as has providing marshy breeding areas for northern pike. Northern pond owners may trigger a winter fish-kill by covering the ice with sand, cutting off light and photosynthesis, which supposedly kills the smaller "trash" fish. This can backfire, however, eliminating forage feed for game fish and possibly increasing summer algal levels.

Physical removal is one of the most effective control methods, especially in relatively small ponds. This is usually accomplished with a partial drawdown and follow-up seining of the unwanted fish. Bass will also have an easier time preying on forage fish if the pond is drawn down enough to eliminate shallow hideaways. Drawdowns have also proven effective at removing carp, by draining water when it's at spawning temperature and exposing the eggs. Drawdowns are most effective if the pond contains a deep pool where the fish can be corralled for seining.

As a last resort, unwanted fish can be poisoned. Powdered rotenone, a naturally derived substance, is usually recommended. When used carefully, it has a relatively brief toxic effect, and some claim that in small doses it can be targeted against smaller forage fish without killing more desirable game species. Aquaculture specialists recommend applying rotenone prior to spawning of valued fish, or after spawning of undesirable species. In general, however, experts warn against using rotenone to target specific species and suggest that the safest use is in a drawn-down pool to kill fish not previously removed. Drawdowns reduce the amount of rotenone required and ensure against an overflow of poison into the downstream watershed.

Because I would never use poison in my own pond, I cannot in good conscience recommend it to others. When people ask me how to get rid of fish, I recommend seining them out, or doing a complete drawdown. However the unwanted fish are killed, they should be removed and buried. Leaving dead fish in a pond will eventually create a nutrient load with alga-producing potential.

Finally, it's important to have a plan for the restored pond. If you decide to restock, make sure to include the correct ratio of game and forage fish. If you simply want a clear-water pond for swimming, keep the bottom-feeding fish out entirely.

See *Drawdown, Rotenone,* and *Seining.*

Fish Traps

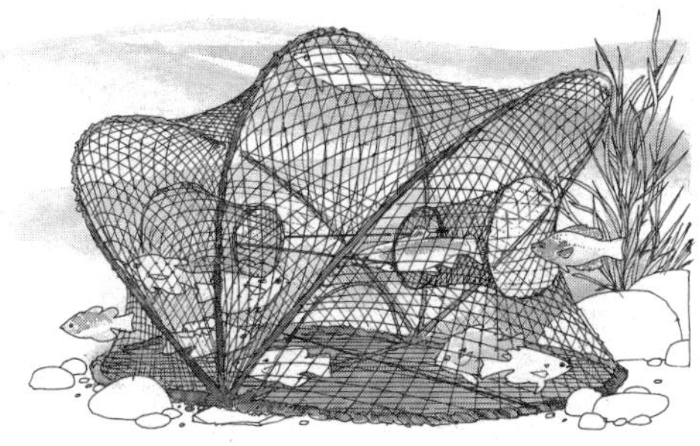

Fish traps are useful for small fish farm harvests or gathering wild minnows for forage feed or bait.

Various trapping devices are used by pond owners for harvest, bait, sampling, removal, and so on, and in some situations to replace seines. Traps range in size and design depending on target species and construction material (plastic, galvanized wire). Larger traps are often collapsible for storage. Traps for minnows and crawfish are popular for catching bait fish. Traps are also available for snakes and eels, and shrimp. Many traps can be fitted with escape doors to comply with regional regulations.

Flood Frequency

U.S. Weather Bureau maps and charts have been compiled showing the average amount of rainfall expected in a given region as well as estimates of the frequency of flooding. Flood frequency is measured in 10-, 25-, and 50-year periods, the higher rainfalls expected over the longer time spans. Flood frequency data can be used to determine the design of pond spillways. Watershed runoff figures (size, slope, vegetation) and pond size are combined with flood frequency potential to determine the maximum overflow a spillway system should be built to handle. In general, the larger the pond and watershed, the larger the spillway capacity should be. Often, it is understood that pipe spillways cannot be economically designed to handle maximum flood runoff, and emergency spillways are also incorporated in the pond design. Flood frequency maps and data for calculating spillway capacity are available from your local Natural Resources Conservation Service office.

See *Spillways*.

Flooding

If a pond's spillway system is unable to discharge sufficient inflow due to high precipitation, runoff, or blocked spillways, flooding may occur. The pond fills until the dam or shore is inundated and water overtops the structure. Such flooding can lead to structural damage to the pond as well as flood damage downstream. Structural damage may include eroded overflow channels and piping, and damage to the shore area or dam. In some cases erosion around piping or in overflow channels may lead to destruction of the dam. The potential for flooding can be minimized in several ways. Pipe spillways and emergency spillways should be designed to discharge high-precipitation events (10-, 25-, or 50-year floods, depending on the size of the pond and watershed). Embankment ponds vulnerable to flooding should be constructed with sufficient freeboard to prevent overtopping. Excavated ponds should be constructed with an elevated shore area to act as a berm to prevent flooding. Upstream berms can also be constructed to deflect flooding. Overflow channels and piping should be checked periodically to prevent blockage by debris, beavers, and the like.

See *Flood Frequency*.

Fountains

Aerial water sprays create a dramatic visual focus for private ponds and at public and commercial installations (golf courses, hotels and resorts, condominiums). Depending on the nozzle used, spray effects include geysers, multiple jets, carousel cascades, and more. Optional lighting units add a liquid fireworks effect at night. Fountains can improve dissolved oxygen levels and water circulation, although they're much less efficient than units designed specifically for aeration. (Those that draw water from the pond or lake bottom tend to be more effective at water circulation than surface pumps.) Electrical costs can be high,

Fountains do double duty as aerators and water features.

and water sprayed into the air during summer days can increase water temperature. Fountains usually require an electrical line run through the water, which may create a safety issue. Where appearance is at a premium, however, there's no denying that a fountain dramatizes the waterscape.

Freeboard

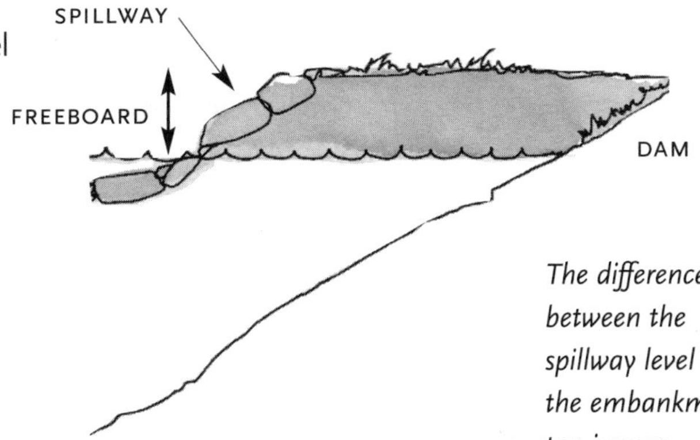

The difference between the spillway level and the embankment top is your insurance against flooding.

The vertical distance between the pond water level at the emergency spillway and the top of the dam. Traditional USDA/Soil Conservation Service pond designs often incorporated as much as 3 feet of freeboard, especially in embankment ponds, as a precaution against overtopping during high-precipitation/runoff events. Excavated ponds without dams, which depend on groundwater, usually require less freeboard. Current pond designers tend to reduce unattractive high freeboard levels by maximizing outlets and emergency spillways and by sloping dams more gently down to the waterline. In watersheds with large acreage and high runoff potential, high freeboard may be necessary.

See *Brimful Effect.*

Frost Level

In northern climates the depth to which the ground freezes will vary depending on location. Knowing your frost level is important in determining how deeply water piping should be buried to prevent freezing or frost heaving. In general, buried outflows should be installed below frost level to prevent heaving and leakage from ice damage. Dry hydrant intake and other kinds of subterranean pond piping (outflow or inflow) should also be buried below frost level. Some pond owners use flexible piping for irrigation and so forth, which they roll up and put away before winter to avoid ice damage; if piped water systems are only needed in summer, burying pipe may be unnecessary.

See *Dry Hydrant*.

Gate Valve

Pond drains require a shut-off fixture. Some builders use a cap or jury-rig a piece of marine plywood sealed with tar or silicone, although a gate valve is preferable (and somewhat more expensive). Two basic types of gate valves are best suited for pond drains. A flap gate is a flat, hinged cover fitted with an adjustable collar that closes over the end of the drainpipe. As the pond fills, water pressure keeps the gate closed, and a gasket or sealant prevents leaks. A rope or chain is attached to the gate, which must be pulled to open. A flap gate is pretty much an all-or-nothing affair, because once the gate is open and water begins to flow, it's difficult if not impossible to close securely before all the water runs out. Caps, plywood, and flap gates are usually used on drains incorporated into standpipe overflow systems.

When more control over drainage flow is required, a valved gate is used. This system usually requires installing a drainpipe independent of a standpipe overflow. The drain is laid through the embankment, with anti-seep collars, and fitted with a valve and riser pipe. By lowering a key wrench into the riser and turning the valve, the operator can open and shut the drain, as well as control flow volume. Valved drain gates make it possible to do partial drawdowns for algal and vegetation control, fish harvests, and repairs; slow drainage also means less erosion, siltation, and fish habitat disruption downstream.

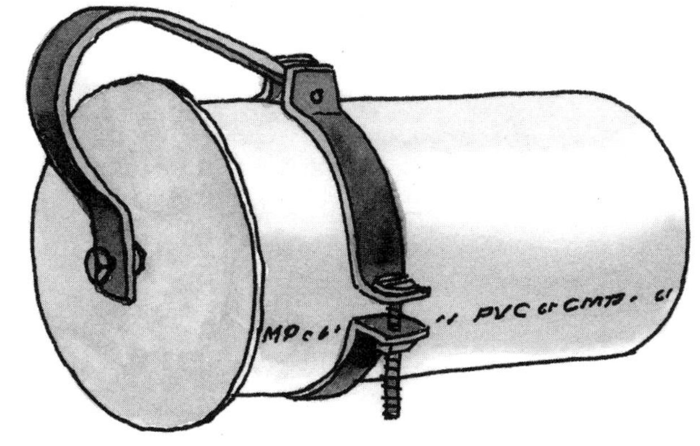

Hinged shut-off used on pond drains, usually controlled by a chain or rope.

Valved drains are more expensive than flap gates—and the extra pipe and installation add to the cost—but increasing numbers of pond owners are making the investment because of the advantages of precision water-level control. (Keep in mind that drains of any kind will be impossible in excavated ponds in flat terrain.)

See *Drain* and *Spillways*.

Geese

Ponds can be used for raising domestic geese and attracting wild migratory varieties. Domestic geese are profitably raised for sale live or for the table, as well as for their down. Wild geese can be attracted to a pond as a wildlife habitat, for hunting, or both. Wild geese are attracted to ponds offering food and cover, which can be cultivated intentionally (millet, wild rice, cattails, and the like). They may also find lawns appetizing and become a serious pest problem.

See *Bird Damage Control, Moist-Soil Management,* and *Waterfowl.*

Geothermal Ponds

Geothermal energy uses the ground temperature of the earth or water for heating, cooling, and producing hot water. Because the ground temperature stays about 50 degrees F year-round, well water or liquid circulated in a buried, closed-loop system can be converted by heat exchange to hot air in winter and cool air in summer. Geothermal energy can save as much as 60 percent on utility bills and eliminate burning of fossil fuels on site.

One of the most economical geothermal systems uses ponds as an energy source. Loops of flexible plastic piping are submerged in the water and connected to a heat exchanger in the house. The "pond loops" are filled with water and nontoxic antifreeze and continuously recirculated between the house and the pond. The connecting pipes are trenched and buried below frost level. In winter the heat exchanger extracts heat from the water, which is used for forced-air heating; in summer the flow is reversed to provide cooling. In addition to residential use, geothermal ponds are being used in resorts, factories, and hospitals. Mandatory detention ponds for condominiums can be attractively landscaped and used for geothermal heating and cooling.

Ponds used for geothermal energy should be ½ acre or larger and at least 8 feet deep. Otherwise heat rejected during summer may overheat the pond, creating lethal habitat for fish and other aquatic critters. To prevent flooding and keep trenching, pumping, and piping costs economical, geo-exchange technicians recommend against using ponds located above a residence or more than 300 feet away.

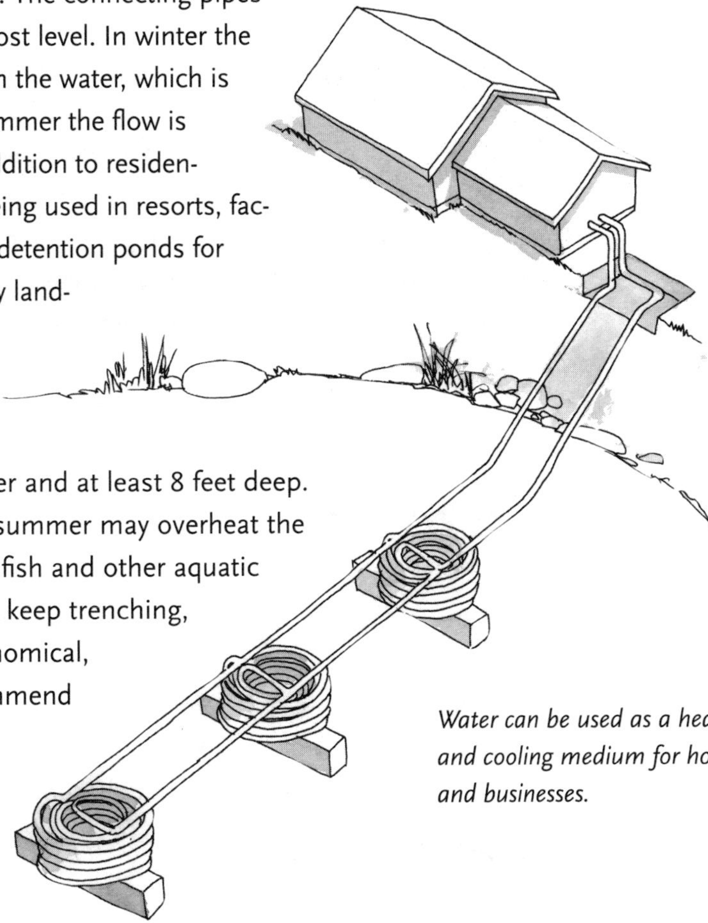

Water can be used as a heating and cooling medium for homes and businesses.

Gley

Gley functions like clay to seal ponds against leakage. Gley is a homemade pond-lining material composed of grass cuttings and other green vegetation packed 6 to 8 inches thick in the pond basin and then compacted by foot, farm animal, or roller. The gley is allowed to sit for a couple of weeks to rot, forming a gel, which holds water. A traditional pond-lining material in developing countries, gley has been popularized in the United States by the New Alchemy Institute, a pioneer in sustainable energy and aquaculture.

See *Liners*.

Goldfish

A member of the carp family often stocked in small garden pools. Goldfish can become a serious problem when stocked in larger ponds because they outcompete other fish for food, cause turbidity, and overpopulate. A few goldfish innocently dropped into a pond often end up requiring a complete drawdown and cleanup. On the plus side, they can help control aquatic algae.

See *Water Gardens* and *Koi*.

Grass Carp

Algae and some aquatic plants may be controlled naturally, without the use of toxic chemicals, by stocking grass carp. Also known as *white amur,* grass carp can graze up to two or three times their body weight in vegetation (algae and rooted plants) every day. Sterile varieties should be used to limit the grass carp population and ensure against non-native species populating public waters. As bottom feeders, grass carp are likely to cause turbid conditions in the water and may adversely affect game fish as well as stimulate additional algal growth with their waste matter. For these reasons, many states prohibit the importation of grass carp. Pond owners should familiarize themselves with stocking and management recommendations before using grass carp.

See *Biological Aquatic Plant Management* and *Crawfish.*

Gravity Feed

Nature's way of moving water for free. Pond inflow systems often take advantage of gravity to deliver water from upstream waterways, springs, wells, or other water bodies. Gravity feed can also be used to move water downhill from a pond for irrigation, livestock water, or other uses. Water can be moved through ditches or piping. Water pressure at a pipe outlet will depend on the head (vertical distance between intake and outflow) and pipe size. Gravity-feed systems are sometimes constructed with air vents along the line to prevent air locks, which can slow down or stop flow, and for line flushing.

See *Vent.*

Guarantee

Pond contractors are not likely to guarantee digging a leakproof pond unless they're also installing a liner. Like well drillers, who also deal with the unknowns of groundwater and make no promises, pond builders can't predict water quality or quantity with 100 percent accuracy. Still, good contractors should do enough preliminary preparation work (test pits, soil tests, land survey, and the like) to feel confident that the project has a good chance of success, as well as spell out the steps they would take to correct unforeseen problems (need for supplementary water, sediment and algal control, leak repair, and so on). In my experience, no contractors worth their salt want to come back again and again to a troubled pond, and they'll do their best to get it right or not take the job. The best way to find that kind of builder is to check out the neighborhood ponds, ask for recommendations, find out which ponds work best and who built them, and check references. The contractor you choose might not guarantee a full pond year-round, but I wouldn't hesitate to ask for a guarantee of craftsmanship.

Arrangements for cost and payment will vary according to contractor. Some may bid the job for a contract price and ask for a down payment up front, another installment at the halfway mark, and a final payment upon completion. Others, knowing how often plans can change when folks see they've got a bulldozer to play with, may prefer to bill by the hour for completed work. Whatever the arrangement, the deal should be clear to both parties up front.

Gypsum

A mineral consisting of hydrous calcium sulfate sometimes used to clarify turbid ponds. Various forms of gypsum are used in sheetrock and plaster of paris. Agricultural gypsum, a soil amendment, can be used to help precipitate suspended particles of clay, which cloud pond water. Finely ground agricultural gypsum is usually applied directly to turbid water, from shore or from a boat, at a rate of approximately 1 ton per acre. The gypsum works by discharging electrical currents in the clay, which prevent fine particles from settling. Other minerals that can be used to precipitate turbid water include agricultural limestone and some commercial fertilizers. Hay, dried or green, may also precipitate turbid ponds.

See *Barley Straw* and *Turbidity*.

Hard Water

Characterized by the presence of dissolved mineral salts (such as calcium or magnesium) that prevent lathering with soap. In ponds and other aquatic systems, adequate hardness is important to newly hatched fish, which obtain much of their calcium from the water. If alkalinity is too high, however, calcium does not dissolve well, so hardness and alkalinity should be in balance.

See *Alkalinity, Soft Water,* and *Water Tests.*

Herons

Migratory wading birds that prey on fish and other aquatic wildlife. Several species of varying size and coloration are widely distributed around the United States and can be a problem for fish farmers and pond owners. Professional aquaculturists may use a variety of elaborate protective measures to prevent predation, including scare-away devices and netting. Amateur fish growers are more likely to suffer losses less grudgingly, appreciative of the privilege of supporting these magnificent birds. Simple strategies such as minimizing shallow edges, providing protective fish cover (floating rafts, habitat), and stocking larger fish can help. Like the kingfisher, these fish-eating birds are a protected species and cannot be trapped or shot.

See *Bird Damage Control.*

Hood Inlet

A pipe spillway that runs straight through embankment, at a slight downward angle, cut or fitted with an elbow to create an opening similar to a drop inlet. These spillways are less expensive than T-risers, cannot incorporate a drain, and in freezing weather may be susceptible to frost damage. They may be fitted with an anti-vortex device (splitter) to prevent erosion around the inlet.

See *Anti-Vortex Device.*

Hydraulic Ram

Using the energy of falling water as a power source, these simple pumps deliver water uphill, almost magically, above the water source. No electricity or wind required! Relatively inexpensive and simple to install, with only a couple of moving parts, they need little maintenance and can be moved easily. Rams are often used to fill ponds from streams or wells located below the pond site. The requirements for a successful ram installation are sufficient vertical fall below the water source and flow volume.

The ram consists of a drive pipe running downhill from the water source to a valve that allows water to discharge until enough pressure accumulates to close the valve. The water is then diverted to a chamber where air pressure rises until

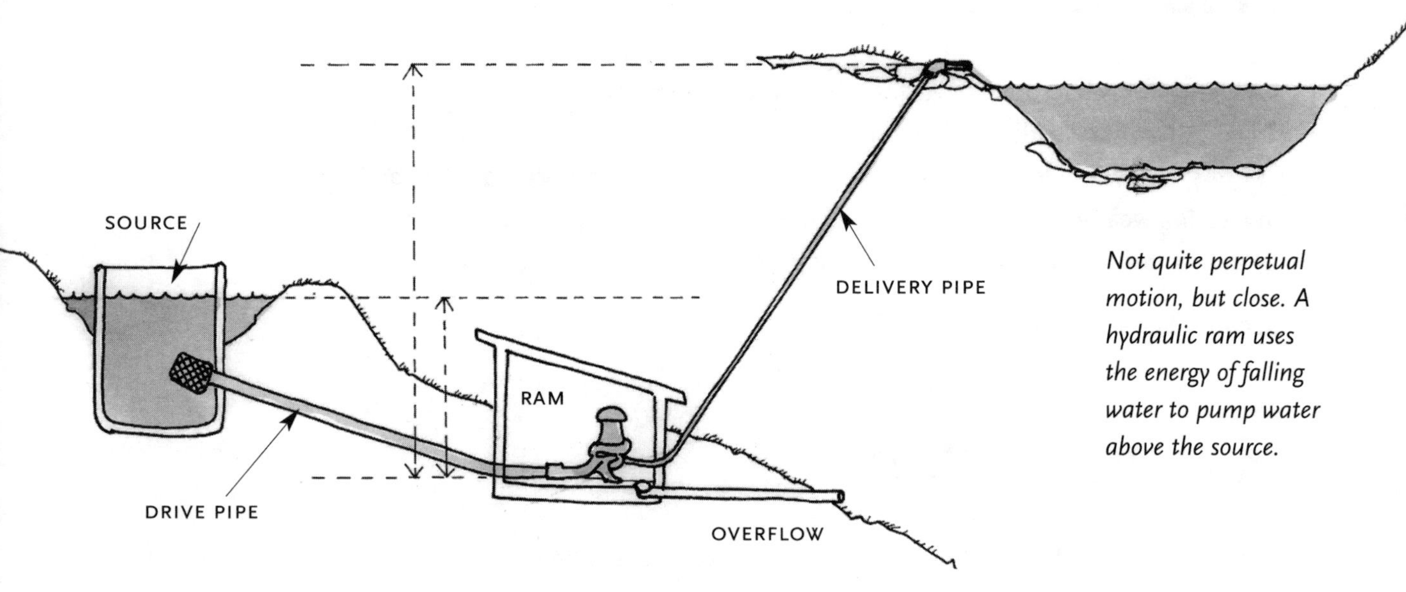

Not quite perpetual motion, but close. A hydraulic ram uses the energy of falling water to pump water above the source.

the compressed air acts like a piston, ramming a squirt of water up a delivery pipe. Then the cycle starts again. Eventually water in the delivery pipe rises above the level of the water source to the discharge point. Because water is lost in the first stage of the hydraulic process, only a percentage of the total flow is rerouted uphill—between 2 and 30 percent, depending on the installation. Rams use drive pipes ranging from 3/4 inch to 3 inches in diameter; they require vertical falls of at least 18 inches and minimum flows of about 2 gallons per minute. Delivery lift and volume will vary depending on the source, pipe size, and length of fall. Rams can lift water as much as 500 vertical feet above a water source.

The first self-acting ram was developed more than 200 years ago by the French pioneer inventor and balloonist Joseph Montgolfier, and they've been used since then to supply water for homes, farms, and municipal systems. A friend of mine uses a ram to move water from a spring below his house to a water tank in his attic, enabling him to enjoy gravity-flow water throughout the house.

Before choosing the ram size, it's important to determine the available flow, as well as the length of pipe from the water source to the ram, and the ram to the delivery point. Keep in mind that flow rates may be less during drier months of the year. Some installations couple multiple rams together to take advantage of variable annual flows. During low-flow periods, some of the rams can be turned off.

Rams are not noise-free; some are quieter than others. And provision should be made for discharge water at the pump. As one supplier notes, "Rams splash big time!"

See *Pumps*.

Hydro Ponds

Hydropower has been used for centuries to generate power. Consider nostalgic images of old New England millponds using water power to press cider, saw lumber, and grind flour, or, later, larger industrial symbols: giant reservoirs with overflow turning electric turbines for utility companies. Most recently, developments in efficient small-scale hydroelectric turbines have made it possible to use backyard ponds for residential electricity.

The two basic considerations for hydropower planning are *head* and *flow*. Head is the vertical distance the water falls from the source to the generating turbine, and flow is the volume of water used to turn the turbine. Traditional systems use low head/high flow to generate large amounts of power. In addition to requiring a lot of water, these systems demand expensive equipment and engineering work. Small-scale hydro systems take advantage of smaller flows combined with high head to generate electricity.

Micro hydro systems generally require between 20 and 100 feet of head and 3 to 100 gallons per minute of flow. Depending on the residential power requirement, these hydro systems can supply all or part of a household's needs. Often, micro hydro setups are used in combination with photovoltaic panels and/or gas generators, which provide backup power when water flow drops in summer.

Micro hydro installations often depend on a year-round stream for water, but pond-construction techniques can be used to create an efficient catchment pool

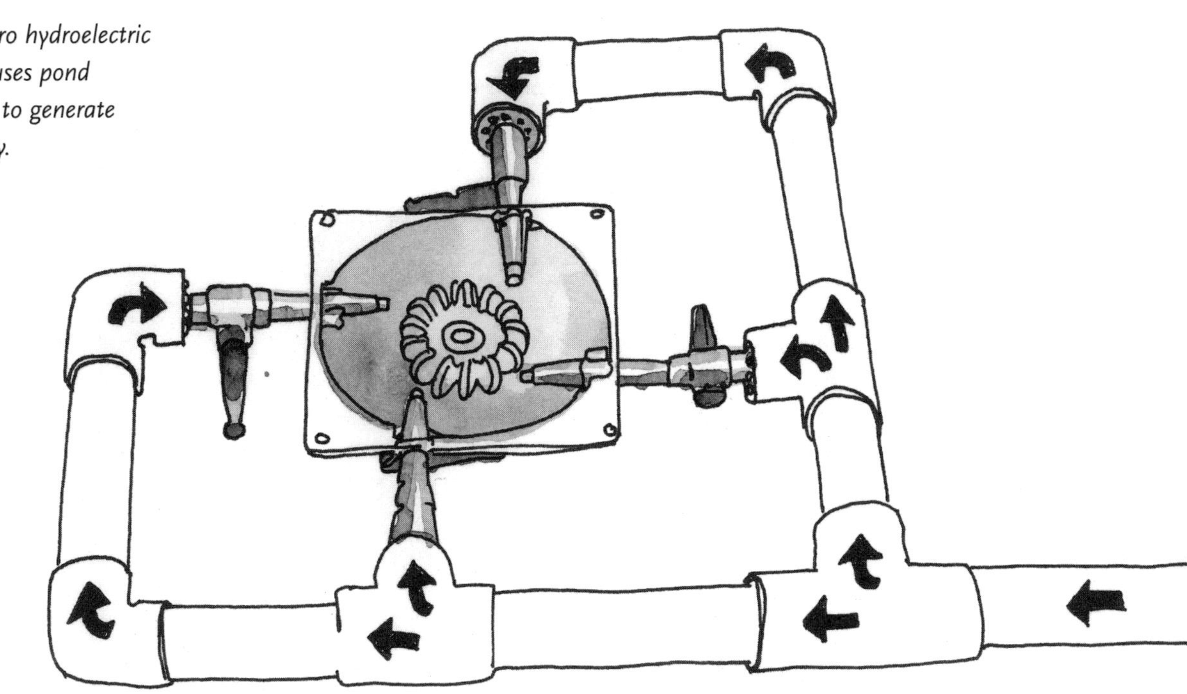

This micro hydroelectric turbine uses pond overflow to generate electricity.

for the intake, or penstock, pipe. "Digger ponds" can be installed in the stream, using notched dams to create a waterfall that carves out an intake pool. Falling water keeps the pool relatively free of silt, preventing clogged pipes.

Larger ponds can also be used to store water for hydro systems. These ponds are usually sited on a hillside, fed by streams and springs, with a dam to impound water. The intake pipe should be installed deep enough below the high-water mark to make water available during low-precipitation periods. The pipe should be carefully installed and protected with anti-seep collars, especially if installed through the dam. The intake should be protected against siltation and clogging, with protective screening to prevent silt particles from clogging the turbine nozzles. In areas where freezing is a problem, the pipe should be buried below frost level. A shut-off valve should be installed near the pond to allow for repairs. Often a vent is installed in the line to allow the operator to "burp" the system in case of air locks. Installing a Y and valve at the turbine allows the operator to flush the line periodically, to remove silt. A pressure gauge helps determine friction loss in the pipe.

It's important to measure the available flow from the pond to determine turbine and pipe size. Keep in mind that it may be impossible to create a system that will run during extreme low-precipitation periods; a backup generating system may be needed. If the pond is drawn down completely, fish habitat may be eliminated, unless the pond is designed to preserve some storage capacity.

Hydrostatic Pressure

Water is heavy: 62.4 pounds per cubic foot. As a pond fills, the weight of the water bearing on the pond can have an effect on water retention. On the one hand, hydrostatic pressure may compact and tighten the pond bed seal. Unfortunately, it can also build up to a point where water is pressurized out through pervious soil, or fissures in ledge. This may explain why some pond water levels mysteriously drop to a certain point and then hold.

Ice

Northern ponds that ice over in winter offer both challenges and rewards to the pond owner. Ice can damage piping systems that have not been properly installed. Riser pipes in deep water are vulnerable to ice damage: as ice forms and shifts, it can loosen or break joints, leading to leaks; damage to the pond structure may follow, especially in spring. Horizontal overflow pipes at water level are often heaved by frost and ice, leading to leakage around the pipe, erosion, and sometimes serious structural damage. Where ice is a potential problem, riser pipes should be installed close to the shoreline where they can be reinforced with earth. Anti-seep collars may prevent ice damage to horizontal water-level overflows, but the safest bet is to avoid them completely.

Ice skating can be one of the great pleasures offered by a backyard pond, but care should be taken not to skate on thin ice (4 inches is generally considered safe). Still, thickness can vary, especially near inflows and outflows and underwater springs, where skating should be avoided. Ponds with water levels that drop in winter often create an unsupported ice shell, which can also be a hazard.

Less than a century ago, pond ice was a natural resource harvested for refrigeration on farms and for commercial sale. Ice-cutting demonstrations are now a feature of winter festivals throughout the North, but there's not much talk of using ice again commercially.

One practical use for pond ice does exist: as a platform for dispersing water conditioners. Pond owners in the North who wish to add agricultural limestone or other conditioners to the water sometimes spread them on the ice. When the ice melts in spring, the substance drops evenly throughout the pond. Sand, which is used for beach areas and as a mulch against aquatic vegetation, can also be ice-dropped. Keep in mind, however, that adding limestone or sand to the ice cuts out sunlight and may adversely affect fish, which depend on oxygen produced by photosynthesis. In fact, by themselves, ice and snow reduce sunlight and may cause fish-kills, especially in actively farmed ponds. Fish farmers sometimes use aeration or snow clearing to preserve healthy oxygen levels. Ice can also create a useful platform for shoreline tree work and removal from hard-to-reach areas.

STAYING SAFE: These ice-thickness safety guidelines were developed by the American Pulpwood Association. They apply to clear, hard ice over still water. To be safe, experienced ice fishers add 2 inches:

- ☞ For one person on foot: 2 inches.
- ☞ For a group of people: 4 inches.
- ☞ For a light car: 7½ inches.
- ☞ For a light truck: 8 inches.
- ☞ For a heavy truck: 10 inches.

Inflow

A general term covering pond water sources: streams, watershed runoff, intermittent veins, springs and piped sources from drainage systems, waterways, and wells.

Invasive Exotic Plants

As long as people have been traveling and migrating, they've taken plants with them for food, medicine, ornamentation, and construction material. While most newly introduced plants don't cause a problem in their new habitat, some do. A vigorous plant with no natural competitors can wreak havoc on native vegetation. Plants such as purple loosestrife, native to Europe, have outcompeted many native North American plants, eliminating habitat and food essential to native wildlife.

Invasive aquatic plants are especially efficient at spreading along rivers and through watersheds, as well as being dispersed by people. Eurasian water milfoil is an aggressive aquatic invader that arrived 50 years ago in North America as an ornamental aquatic plant and spread into lakes, rivers, and ponds when people emptied their aquariums into local waters. Other aquatic invasive plants such as water chestnut and hydrilla are spreading from decorative water gardens and aquariums into larger water bodies. Without quarantines and controls on invasive exotic plants, our native waters are vulnerable to being overrun, curtailing recreation and displacing native plants and wildlife.

See *Eurasian Water Milfoil.*

Irrigation Ponds

Agriculture wouldn't exist without a reliable source of water, and for many farmers and gardeners, that source is a pond. In fact, pond construction began because of the need for irrigation, and it's changed little over thousands of years. Farmers calculate how much water a certain amount of acreage will require over the growing season and dig a pond with a corresponding capacity. Irrigation ponds may have different sources: seasonal runoff, springs, streams, or water piped in from another source. The earliest ponds took advantage of muscle power (animal or human) or gravity to deliver water to crops. With the development of windpower, piping, and pumps, irrigation was streamlined. Gardeners and farmers today use water pumps powered by gas, electricity (including photovoltaic generated), tractor, wind, and gravity.

Irrigation ponds work best if dug deep, to reduce evaporation during summer when demand is high. Hydrants are sometimes installed to create a reliable, deep intake and simplify connections. Water conservation techniques are often used, such as drip irrigation hoses and night watering. Gardens and fields sited at elevations lower than the pond can eliminate the need for pumping by taking advantage of gravity flow. Spraying is also used to protect against frost and extend the growing season.

See *Drip Irrigation*.

Islands

Many ponds include an island. Most are built during construction of the pond. In a dugout pond they're usually built by leaving an unexcavated area within the structure. Embankment ponds may require a constructed island, usually built with native soil, or occasionally large stones. Islands in shallow areas are easier to build than those in deep water. Bridges are sometimes installed between island and shore. Small islands favored by turtles and other amphibians can be created by installing large boulders, or even logs lying in shallow water. They have the advantage of being removable.

Islands can be used for recreation, aesthetics, and wildlife. Because waterfowl appreciate a predator-free place to rest, feed, and nest, islands are popular in wildlife-oriented ponds.

Islands can also be created during pond cleanouts, using dredged material for construction, saving both the expense of removing dredged material and the cost of buying additional fill. Because this material is often poor-construction-quality silt, these "waste" islands are favored for wildlife habitat.

Islands can be a source of trouble. Those created with "left behind" unexcavated material may lead to leaks if the soil has not been compacted on the top or slopes. Island slopes should be gradual enough to allow for good compaction by construction equipment. Islands also add to the total area of submerged shallows, which may encourage undesired aquatic vegetation as well as higher water temperatures. Islands decrease total water volume, which reduces capacity for fish culture and water storage. I usually advise against island construction except in ponds with an acre or more water surface and plenty of depth.

See *Waterfowl.*

Kingfishers

Predatory birds with a distinctive call (a castanet-like rattle) and a big appetite for fish, which are especially easy prey when confined in a pond. Fish farmers are more likely to experience serious losses from kingfishers because of fish density and may be forced to use predator control methods. Other pond owners may be willing to lose a few fish in support of a vital wild bird population. Wild bird enthusiasts appreciate tree branches near or overhanging a fish pond to attract kingfishers, while those who would prefer to discourage them remove proximate trees and snags. Kingfishers are a federally protected species and cannot be trapped or shot.

See *Bird Damage Control.*

Koi

Multicolored member of the carp family often stocked in decorative water gardens and fish pools. Depending on pedigree and coloring, they can be very expensive.

See *Goldfish* and *Water Gardens.*

Landscaping

Oxymoronic as it may sound, there is such a thing as pond landscaping. Unlike water gardens, which usually focus on aquatic plants, larger earth ponds involve more land-based planting and design. How come? Earth ponds are bigger and deeper than water gardens, making them less suited to the aquatic planting, primping, and preening that go on in water gardens. Besides, who wants to swim through a patch of lotuses and water lilies? Still, focusing attention on the shore doesn't mean you have to noodle every square inch of space with plants and shrubs and trees. Ponds need to breathe.

As with most forms of landscaping, pond landscaping takes its cues from the terrain. Mountains, valleys, plains—all have natural signatures. Ponds have distinct characteristics, too. They can be generally classified into two landforms: excavated and dammed.

Excavated (also called *dugout*) ponds are usually dug in relatively flat terrain, river valleys and fields, while dammed ponds need an embankment to hold water on sloping terrain. Excavated ponds are generally less perplexing landscape projects. The shoreland surrounding the pond is flat, and there's no dam to disguise. Without much effort, the owner can blend the dugout pond into the landscape. In a pasture or meadow, you might simply reseed the shoreland and plant a shade tree or two. Willows show up frequently around ponds, as a single tree or in a row along the shore, and there's no denying their visual charm. These trees are especially popular around excavated ponds, where there's less concern about the potential for root damage to a dam. But willow leaves shedding into a pond often create a mess of their own—vegetative debris and turbid water. Beware. An alternative species may be the wiser if less dramatic choice.

Embankment ponds are more challenging. The nature of the dam itself is unnatural. Mounded on top of already sloping terrain, it can sometimes display all the charm of a gopher hill on steroids. Seen from below (sited above a home or driveway, for instance), it can grab an observer's attention and not let go. A view from above is often better, with water shifting attention from the bulky dam (unless there's too much freeboard).

The embankment soil itself, tightly compacted and high in clay content, is a poor medium for plant growth. It can be a real challenge to establish grass,

Stonework, trees, and aquatic plants transform a roughed out excavation into an attractive pondscape. The key to pond landscaping is to mimic nature.

especially considering the generally accepted prohibition against fertilizer, which would stimulate undesired algal growth and aquatic weeds. Saving topsoil during construction, to spread later on the dam, will help the grass along. Hand raking, conservation seed mixes, and lots of mulch are also important. Sod (and patience) may be required.

Embankment slopes present more challenges. Three-to-one slopes (and sometimes steeper) on the outside face of the dam are vulnerable to erosion, especially right after construction, and should be seeded with a mixture of quick-developing annual and slower-rooting perennial grasses, and then mulched. The slope is often too steep for mowing to be done by hand. Native wildflowers can make an attractive embankment cover as long as you're careful that the soil preparation doesn't compromise soil stability. Planting trees on the embankment is usually cautioned against because of the potential for damaging leaks caused by roots.

The area opposite the embankment can also present problems. Slopes draining into the pond should be protected against erosion, which can damage terrain and lead to siltation in the pond. Slopes often include springs that feed the pond but are too wet and stony to support plants or grass. Underground drain piping may be needed to dry out the soil. Feeder streams should also be protected against erosion and pond siltation. A fieldstone lining in the streambed can be an attractive stabilizing feature. Streamside shrubs and trees adaptable to wet soil will help reinforce the streambank. Species should be matched to your climate zone, as well as being noninvasive.

Most pond owners aim to create a natural-looking landscape (the Victorian emphasis on formal gardens being out of style just now). With new ponds this often involves a combination of imported plants and seeds in some areas and a laissez-faire approach elsewhere to allow native species a chance to become established.

For instance, a south-facing slope overlooking my pond was too steep to leave unplanted after construction. It would have eroded into the pond. So we established some quick-growing grass (a conservation mix protected with mulch) and later seeded the area with blue and purple lupines. Now, every spring, the lupines signal the beginning of swimming season (along with the peepers). We also seeded the hardpacked clay embankment, which took several summers and reseedings to turn green. We planted a privacy hedge of blueberry bushes along the outside edge of the dam. The blueberries needed deep holes full of peat and topsoil to catch on in the hardpacked earth.

On the other hand, the sloping watershed area opposite the embankment was left pretty much on its own. It was too wet to do much with (drainage tiles would have been a possible but expensive corrective), and over the years the native ferns have flourished, as well as a dramatic trio of white birch trees and an ancient apple tree. The slope has a wild aspect that balances off the groomed embankment.

We did establish a groundcover of timothy, rye, and fescue on the embankment, which I now periodically mow, leaving a foot-wide band of native vegetation at the water's edge. It's good cover for small critters (dragonflies, frogs, salamanders), and the sedges that volunteer there are attractive.

A wetland refuge designer once surprised me by saying that he advises builders to import zero plants. "Forget plantings," he said, "the plants will come on their own." I'd expected a laundry list of rushes, cattails, sago, wild rice, and what have you. But his approach was to let Nature do her thing, save the money and effort, and avoid plants that might crash in your habitat.

True, this is a tactic best suited to constructed wetland refuges, where you may not have to worry about aesthetics or erosion, but I've also seen it work at my "recreational" pond. A few years ago, a scattering of tiny wildflowers appeared on the embankment and spread into a pink-and-white quilt that reappears every summer. I wasn't able to identify them in my flower guides until a native-plant expert I know took a look and explained why. The plant was Kalm's lobelia, a wildflower rare in this area, which my books didn't have room for. Recently some tiny orchids began flowering amid the lobelia. "You wouldn't have these plants if you'd been maintaining a traditional lawn and garden," my friend told me.

The laissez-faire landscaping style does have its limits. A few cattails emerged in the shallows a while ago, and if they begin to spread, I'll pull them. I've seen too many ponds taken over by invasive plants. Water needs an occasional weeding, too.

Leaks

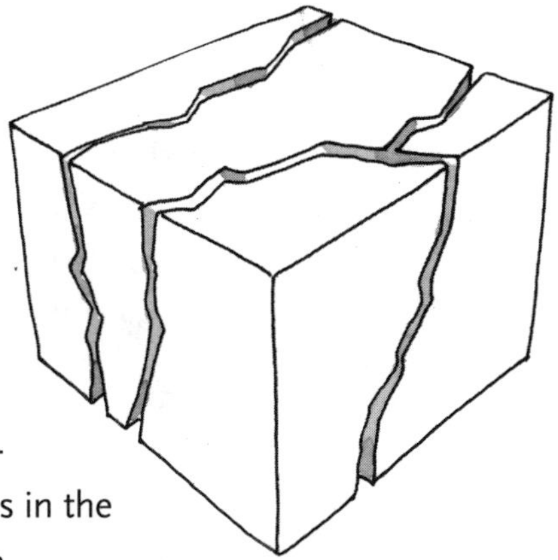

Ponds can leak in all sorts of ways, some rather benign (endurable during short droughty periods when normally adequate inflow doesn't compensate), others serious enough to require repair and/or supplementary water. All earth ponds leak to some degree, unless they're lined with impermeable sheeting or sealant. This is called seepage. It's natural, and in fact when there's sufficient inflow to maintain the water level, it's part of the recharge dynamic that sustains good water quality. Unacceptable seepage is usually due to areas in the pond bed with infiltratable soil that wasn't properly sealed over with a layer of well-compacted clay-rich soil during construction. To fix these kinds of leaks, the pond is usually drained enough to expose the problem area, repaired, and refilled. Finding leaks and seeps can be tricky. If a pond's water level drops to a certain point and then holds, the leak may be somewhere in the vicinity of the waterline. Look for shaley, sandy, gravelly, or ledgey areas, and apply clay, sealant, or liner material. If the leak is in the pond embankment, signs of excessive moisture may appear on the backslope of the dam, near the toe or farther downstream. Rich vegetative growth can also be a clue. The leak itself may be on the inside of the dam, or it might be trickling through the foundation seam or straight down into the pond bed. Leaks can sometimes be traced by sprinkling flour or cream into the water near a suspected leak and looking for signs of it being drawn toward the area in question. Vegetable dyes can also be used to trace leaks. Dye is added to the pond and the exterior is monitored for corre-

Fissures in bedrock can be a source of pond water or leaks, and sometimes both.

spondingly colored streams. Dowsers are also used occasionally to attempt to locate leaks.

Piping systems can cause leakage too. Spillway systems piped through an embankment can leak at the joints, or the pipe itself. Steel or iron is subject to corrosion; plastic can crack. Leaks can also develop around the outside of a pipe, especially without anti-seep collars (seepage around the outside of a spillway outlet may indicate such leakage).

See *Dye* and *Liners.*

Ledge

Large slabs of bedrock, which can obstruct pond construction or cause leaks. Ironically, springs often surface in ledgey areas, tempting builders to site ponds in or near these areas. The spring activity is often seasonal, however, and when flow ceases, fissures in the ledge can funnel water out of the pond. Building dams on a ledge foundation is also risky because of the likelihood of leakage between the ledge and embankment material. Clay or sheet liners, or both, are sometimes used to seal ledgey areas, although they may require underdrains to prevent spring activity from damaging the liner. While I have seen successful ponds constructed near or incorporating ledge, they usually attest more than anything to the builders' good luck.

See *Leaks* and *Liners.*

Leeches

Cousin to the earthworm, this variety of annelid is not welcome in most ponds, where the bloodsucking strains may clamp onto swimmers for a fresh meal. There are more than 50 strains of freshwater leeches in North America, some with teeth, some without. Leeches can be carnivorous, parasitic, or predacious, depending on the species. The bloodsucking horse leech is one of the most familiar pond parasites, often hitchhiking in on the feet of waterfowl or other critters. Another, the black ribbon leech, is a favorite of anglers, who use it to catch game fish.

Although most pond owners now try their best to get rid of leeches, they were once cultured and used medicinally, when it was believed that draining a patient's blood could cure disease. Doctors traveled with attractively designed ceramic leech pots and became known themselves as "leeches." Although not as popular today, leeches continue to be used medically to reduce swelling after injury or surgery. They are also cultured and trapped in the wild and sold as game fish bait.

Leeches tend to do best in shallow northern ponds, where top-to-bottom freezing eliminates the game fish that prey on them. They aren't well adapted to especially acidic waters, or to ponds that dry up in summer, which kills them. A pond full of algae with its related population of amphibians and other critters is an ideal leech habitat.

Pond owners use a variety of tactics to try to eliminate leeches, ranging from toxic chemicals such as copper sulfate and rotenone to more ecofriendly biological controls. The problem with chemicals is that they also kill other aquatic inhabitants, from fish to frogs to plants, and after the chemical disperses, there's nothing to deter a new leech population from immigrating. I've known pond owners to tie a steak to a string and dangle it in the water, occasionally catching a few leeches but rarely solving the problem for long. Bait suppliers who culture and trap leeches use mesh funnels on top of a can baited with fish to trap them, usually after dark; leeches are primarily nocturnal feeders. One pond owner I know has his inflow trickle over a salt lick, claiming it makes the pond saline enough to eliminate leeches, which are freshwater creatures. In my own pond, I solved the leech problem once and for all by stocking crawfish, which eat leeches, as well as algae.

See *Copper Sulfate, Crawfish,* and *Rotenone.*

Levee

An embankment built up to control flooding—either to protect against it or to contain floodwater for irrigation. Often constructed along riverfronts to deflect annual spring floods.

See *Embankment.*

Liability

Depending on the type of pond, its location, and the people involved, pond ownership may make the owner legally liable for injuries or death connected with an "attractive nuisance." The concept of attractive nuisance, often applied to swimming pools, can also apply to ponds. An attractive nuisance is a pool or pond (or other entity) sufficiently accessible and attractive to passersby, especially children, that it may be considered a safety threat. Such ponds and pools may require safety features such as fencing, NO TRESPASSING signs, etc. In general, the more suburban the neighborhood, the more likely it is that a pond will be considered a potential danger. Rural municipalities where ponds are a traditional landscape feature are less likely to classify ponds an attractive nuisance. Pond owners, or anyone considering building a pond, should consult the state attorney's office, and their insurance carrier, to determine if safety precautions and/or extra liability coverage is necessary.

Regardless of legal liability, pond owners should assess the potential for accidents—particularly their pond's proximity and accessibility to children—and take action if necessary. Fencing, NO TRESPASSING signs, shallow slopes, and removal of enticing features (water slides and swings, etc.) have been recommended by authorities.

See *Dam Safety and Liability*.

Limestone (Agricultural)

Sedimentary rock processed into granular form for use as a farm and garden soil amendment. Agricultural limestone raises the pH level and promotes fertility. It's used by pond owners to adjust pH level and increase fertility, especially in fish culture ponds. Limestone is usually added to establish a neutral pH (8 or 9), which is especially useful when raising warm-water fish such as carp, tilapia, and catfish. Limestone helps promote the growth of blue-green algae and plankton, essential to the growth of these fish. Dosage rates will depend on the pond pH, the species being raised, time of year, and pond size. Limestone can be applied dry or as a slurry and is considered nontoxic unless the pH goes over 10. It's also used as a disinfectant in drained fish ponds before refilling. Limestone is sometimes used in wastewater treatment ponds to reduce phosphorous and to improve water quality in lakes affected by storm water runoff.

See *Alkalinity* and *pH.*

Liners

Natural or manufactured bottom barriers used to reduce or eliminate pond seepage or leaks. The earliest pond liners were created by farmers combining straw or grass with manure, which was then tamped into the pond bed by hand or with draft animals packing the surface on hoof and later with rollers. Today

Membrane liners are often installed when native pond soil lacks sufficient clay to hold water.

fish farmers sometimes line infiltratable soils with "gley," a natural sealant composed of grass clippings. Clay liners are often used to reduce seepage in ponds with porous soils; to be effective, wet clay is usually applied at least a foot thick and packed by machine. A layer of crushed stone on top of the clay creates a firm pond bed. Bentonite, a mined clay, is another popular liner material, which is usually purchased dry and disked or rototilled into the dry pond bed before filling. Bentonite and silty clays can cause turbidity when stirred up by swimmers, animals, or fish.

Plastic and rubber membranes are also used to line leaky ponds. Care must be taken to prepare a smooth substrate to prevent sharp stones from puncturing the membrane; sand or blanketing fabric is often used. Sand is often used as a protective cover for membrane liners. Polymer emulsions, liquid rubber, and other soluble materials are also used for lining ponds, especially those with irregular surfaces.

Spring-fed ponds may require drainage systems beneath the liner to prevent erosion of the clay, emulsion, or displacement of the artificial membrane, which will belly-up because of hydrostatic pressure from below.

See *Clays, Gley,* and *Leaks.*

Maintenance

Necessary to guaranteeing pond longevity and performance. There are two basic dimensions to pond maintenance: *water* and *basin structure.* To maintain good water quality, aquatic vegetation should be kept under control to prevent eutrophication. Algae, and submergent and emergent aquatic vegetation, should not be allowed to colonize the pond. Surrounding tree litter can add organic matter to the water, which feeds algae. Trees may need to be thinned or cut back from the shoreline. Water quality, especially temperature and oxygen, should be monitored if fish crops are being raised, particularly during hot summer weather.

To maintain the pond structure, trees should not be allowed to grow on pond embankments because of the potential for leaks due to root damage. Earthen inflow and outflow channels should be monitored for erosion damage, especially in spring and during flooding. Shoreline sedimentation at inflow areas can reduce pond capacity, foster aquatic vegetation, and block inflow pipes; sediment should be removed periodically, and sources of erosion eliminated if possible. In older ponds, sediment throughout the pond can accumulate enough to cause water-quality problems (low oxygen, high temperatures, and the like) and feed algae and pond weeds. Cleanout excavation may be required. Spillway piping should be inspected to ensure against leaks and blockages. If beavers are a problem, protective baffling around spillways should be installed; animal removal may be necessary. Spring is an important season for pond inspection, following snowmelt, thawing, and high-volume runoff. Summer is a good time for repairs, when water levels are low and construction equipment least likely to damage shoreline terrain or get bogged down.

See *Cleanout* and *Erosion*.

Maps

Various maps can be used to aid in the selection of a pond site and in pond design. One of the most helpful is the U.S. Geological Survey (USGS) series of topographic maps, which are available from the Department of Interior and may be found in local sporting goods outlets and other retail outlets, or online. These maps detail contour lines, streams and rivers, and water bodies and are used to calculate the size of the watershed draining into a potential pond site. Using formulas available through the National Resources Conservation Service, the size of the watershed is then used to help determine pond capacity and spillway requirements. The NRCS offers additional maps, charts, and aerial photos that can be used in pond site selection and design. Aerial photos are one of the most useful references in accurately determining watershed acreage. After locating your pond site on the appropriate photograph, a stereoscope and planimeter can be used to determine contour lines and then the size of the drainage area. Soil Survey maps grade soils according to infiltration, which helps determine the holding capacity of the pond (on-site test pits, however, are the gold standard for soil analysis). A continental watershed map shows the drainage area needed to sustain each acre-foot of water. There are also maps of regional minimum pond depths, rainfall distribution, and rainfall frequency. Many of these maps and charts are printed in the NRCS Agricultural Handbook 590, which is a must for every pond builder's library.

See *Watershed.*

Moist-Soil Management

A waterfowl enhancement method for both natural and constructed ponds and wetlands. Waterfowl are attracted to food and cover in natural areas with varying water levels. In the seasonal cycle, pond water levels rise in autumn and winter and drop in summer. Plants germinate as water levels fall, then produce seeds that are later submerged and fed on by dabbling ducks and other waterfowl. Pond owners and wetland managers mimic this cycle by using water control structures to drain basins in summer, allowing volunteer moist-soil plants to grow.

Sometimes cultivated crops such as millet are sown, although natural plants such as smartweed have proved a more nutritious waterfowl food and are better adapted to variable weather and water conditions. In fall the drains are closed and the basins allowed to fill, creating an attractive habitat for migrating waterfowl.

Moist-soil management methods were pioneered by the U.S. Fish and Wildlife Service and conservation organizations such as Ducks Unlimited, which offer information about dewatering systems and techniques, pond and wetland design criteria, and plant recommendations.

See *Constructed Wetlands* and *Water Control Structures.*

Mosquitoes

The water necessary for successful mosquito breeding is generally shallow and stagnant, ranging from puddles to old tires to weedy marshes and wetlands. Ponds with well-sloped shore areas, and especially those containing fish, are not likely to produce mosquitoes. In fact, one of the traditional reasons to build a pond has been to transform a mosquito-infested marsh into a deeper reservoir stocked with fish. Mosquito larvae are a favorite food of fish, reptiles, amphibians, and dragonflies and don't last long in a well-constructed pond. Pond areas where the adult female mosquito can lay her eggs include edge areas with debris and thick stands of submerged aquatic vegetation, which protect larvae from fish and other predators. Where mosquitoes are a problem, these breeding areas should be cleaned up. Mosquito-borne diseases such as malaria and yellow fever have been eliminated in the United States, but the recently introduced West Nile virus is spread by mosquitoes, as is canine heartworm. Ironically, wetland protection laws may limit mosquito control by prohibiting pond construction in marshy areas; where mosquito control is an objective, variances may be allowed. In general, builders and owners should design and maintain ponds to minimize mosquito breeding areas.

Pond owners looking for natural mosquito control report success with gambusia affinis. *In fact, most fish help control mosquitoes.*

See *Biological Insect Pest Control, Detention Ponds,* and *Mosquitofish.*

Mosquitofish

A small minnow ($2\frac{1}{2}$ inches maximum) that feeds in surface strata of water where mosquito larvae hatch, making it an excellent biological control for mosquitoes. It was stocked in shallow waters during construction of the Panama Canal and credited with controlling yellow fever and malaria. Today it is used in many areas of the United States for mosquito control. Tolerant of adverse conditions, including high temperatures, high salinity, and low dissolved oxygen, mosquitofish are prolific breeders and can also be raised for bait. Local fish and wildlife regulations may prohibit mosquitofish in some states because of concerns about damaging natural fish populations.

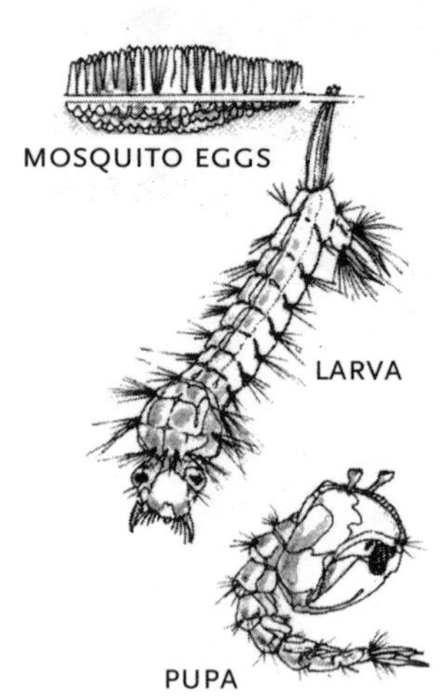

See *Biological Insect Pest Management* and *Mosquitoes.*

Muskgrass is often found in water high in lime, which accounts for its grainy texture.

Muskgrass (Chara)

Submerged algae large enough to pass for a rooted plant. They provide cover for small fish but are usually considered an invasive and unwanted nuisance.

See *Invasive Exotic Plants.*

Muskrats

Pond-dwelling rodents similar to beavers with an appetite for submerged and emergent vegetation and a penchant for den building, although on a reduced scale due to their smaller size. They're well known for their appetite for cattails (for food and building material), as well as other pond plants, making them a threat (or asset, depending on your point of view) to garden pools and ponds alike. The burrows they may dig in pond sides can lead to leaks or cave-ins, and their waste matter may contaminate swimming ponds.

These burrowing rodents can damage embankments and may have to be removed.

Control techniques include eliminating protective cover and edible vegetation (especially cattails), and trapping. Some pond owners install a layer of riprap or galvanized wire mesh along shore to a depth of 3 feet below the surface and a foot above. Electric fencing is another option. (A similar rodent, the nutria, was introduced from South America and presents comparable problems in the southern United States.)

See *Beavers.*

Natural Resources Conservation Service (NRCS)

A federal agency under the U.S. Department of Agriculture, formerly the Soil Conservation Service. Agents in district offices help implement a variety of conservation-oriented programs for private landowners. Many of their services and programs can be useful for pond owners and builders, including soil surveys, watershed surveys and planning, flood prevention, wetlands operations, and wildlife habitat improvement. It's well worth a call to your county NRCS office before embarking on a pond construction or improvement project—or visit the group's web site (www.nrcs.gov).

Nets

One of the most essential tools in the fish farmer's stockpile. Various nets are used for catching and corralling fish, and protecting them from predators. Hand nets, casting nets, and seines are used to gather fish. Netting is used to build floating cages for cage culture. Fish benefit from protective shade made from netting. Nets are also used as leaf skimmers and bags for collecting invasive weeds underwater.

See *Cage Culture, Predators,* and *Seines.*

Nitrate

A chemical compound representing final stage in decay of ammonia, nitrate is used as a plant nutrient. It's not usually considered a threat to freshwater fish, although it may trigger algal blooms, especially in water gardens. Levels can be determined with water-quality test strips and kits.

See *Water Tests.*

Nitrite

A chemical compound formed in the oxidation process of ammonia, which can damage fish by interfering with oxygen absorption. Toxic levels are usually found in recirculating fish ponds with inadequate filtration or a lack of fresh water. Levels can be determined with water-quality test strips and kits.

See *Water Tests.*

Nitrogen

A relatively inert element that in gas form constitutes 78 percent of the atmosphere. In rare cases nitrogen may contribute to water-quality problems because of oversaturation due to flawed water pumping, aeration, well water, or overheating (usually detected by fish-kills or "popeye" disease). Other products of the nitrogen cycle (ammonia, nitrite, nitrate) are more likely to degrade water quality due to contaminated runoff entering a pond (fertilizer, wastewater), as well as the decay of plant life and fish waste. Nitrogen and its compounds are of special interest to water gardeners working with closed systems.

See *Ammonia, Nitrate, Nitrite,* and *Water Tests.*

Overflow

Any discharge of water in excess of pond capacity that overflows through spillway systems: piping, earth-cut channels, gates control, boxes, and so forth. Overflow is normally a beneficial process because high-quality water is usually enhanced by a continuous exchange (inflow/outflow) of fresh water.

See *Spillways.*

Oxygen

The most abundant element on earth and essential to most forms of life. Normally oxygen makes up about 90 percent of water, but levels vary according to conditions in and around the water. When levels drop too low, the health of aquatic plants and animals is at risk. Oxygen is measured in units of dissolved oxygen (DO), in parts per million (ppm), and milligrams per liter (mg/l). DO levels in a pond usually range between 1 ppm and 8 ppm, depending on the time of day, and light levels. Photosynthesis of submerged plants produces oxygen, meaning that oxygen levels will rise during sunny daylight hours and drop during the night. Other factors affecting DO levels include temperature (higher temperatures create conditions that use up and lower DO), respiration (decaying organic matter uses up oxygen), water velocity (anything that agitates the water, from wind to stream activity, mixes oxygen into the water), depth (DO levels generally drop the deeper you go), groundwater inflow (DO levels in springwater are low, although the cool temperatures eventually help raise levels), and season (DO levels drop as photosynthesis declines in winter, then rise with increasing sunlight). If water quality or fish health suffers, DO levels should be checked and, if needed, aeration used to raise oxygen content. Aeration can raise DO levels by natural or mechanical means. Photosynthesizing plants can be introduced and are valued by water gardeners. Inflows of fresh water splashing into a pond help raise DO. Mechanical systems can aerate the water by recirculation, splash pumps, compressed air, and other systems.

See *Aeration* and *Water Tests.*

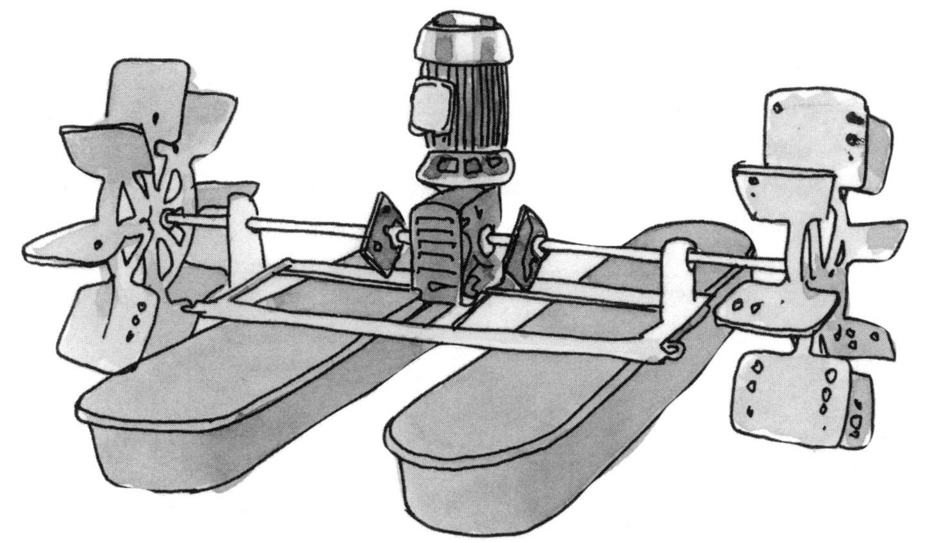

It looks like an airboat, which in a way it is. The paddlewheel aerator is designed to splash large, quick doses of life-giving oxygen into oxygen-poor ponds.

Paddle-Wheel Aerator

A splash aerator that can quickly add oxygen to large area of a pond and is especially useful in halting fish-kills. Paddle-wheels can be mounted on a trailer and powered by tractor drive, so the aerator is mobile and can be moved to specific locations service different ponds. Not designed for economical long-term operation but valued by fish farmers for emergency use.

See *Aeration.*

Peat

Partially decomposed vegetative matter, especially spaghnum moss, found in bogs. Often intentionally dredged out of wetlands for use as an additive to gardening soil and for insulation and fuel. Many ponds excavated in wetlands have produced peat products, although recent environmental regulations against wetland destruction in the United States have limited the peat industry. Peat bogs are valuable wetland environments, often supporting wildlife and rare plants. It's worth noting that these bogs contain peat as deep as 40 feet and to create a stable pond structure all of the peat would have to be removed—another good reason to leave these bogs alone.

See *Wetlands.*

Perforated Pipe

Rigid plastic pipe with holes, installed underground to gather and move water out of a saturated area, for drainage purposes. Can be useful in watersheds upslope of a pond to dry out terrain. Also used to collect groundwater and runoff to feed downhill into a pond. Often wrapped in geotextile fabric and backfilled with crushed stone to prevent sediment clogging.

See *Drainage Field.*

Permitting

In an ever-more-regulated land, ponds are no exception. Because of the federal Clean Water Act of 1972 (and subsequent revisions), wetlands are considered a protected environmental asset, and—depending on a specific wetland's classification—any alteration is prohibited without a permit. State laws also regulate wetlands. Many sites that in the past would have been considered natural pond locations are now off-limits. Still, depending on wetland classification and pond size, small wetlands may be approved for excavation. Various other state and local laws may also regulate pond construction details (embankment, volume, spillway piping, and more). The bottom line: before digging a pond, make sure to comply with all relevant laws. More than one pond has been filled back in because it was built without a permit.

See *Wetlands.*

pH

Along with dissolved oxygen and temperature, pH is one of the most important factors in determining water quality. It's a measure of acidity and alkalinity in a solution. On a scale of 0 to 14, the number 7 represents neutrality. Lower numbers indicate increasing acidity, and higher numbers represent increasing alkalinity (each unit of change marks a tenfold increase). Knowing a pond's pH can

pH tests range from simple litmus paper strips to highly accurate chemical kits.

be important in judging water quality for fish culture and general ecological health. In general, a pH of between 5 and 8 is considered acceptable for most fish species. Factors that can trigger extremes in pH include acid precipitation (acidity) and ammonia (alkalinity). pH can be measured by using litmus paper or more sophisticated metering devices.

See *Water Tests.*

Phosphorous (P)

A mineral that in pure form is poisonous and flammable but does not occur naturally in uncombined form. In compound, phosphorous is found in many minerals and commercial products (phosphates), especially fertilizer and detergents. It is present naturally in plants and animals and released during decay. Added to ponds, P often triggers growth of plants, especially algae, which can lead to water-quality problems, oxygen depletion, and eutrophication. P management is an important element in pond maintenance. Control begins with preventing addition from runoff (usually agricultural or commercial fertilizer, septic, or storm water) as well as biological removal (aeration, bacterial decay), precipitation, inactivation, and physical removal.

See *Water Tests.*

Polyculture

A mutually beneficial, highly efficient food chain, where fish feed on plant growth nourished by bird waste.

Use of ponds to raise more than one crop at a time, often with one species benefiting another. For example, a crop of carp can be raised along with a flock of waterfowl (ducks or geese). Waste matter from the birds fertilizes aquatic vegetation, which in turn sustains the fish. Waste matter from livestock can also be used to fertilize fish ponds in polyculture systems. Polyculture is a highly economical, sustainable system that has been used by farmers for many centuries.

See *Fish Ponds, Pond Rotation,* and *Waterfowl.*

Pond

Derived from the Old English word *pound,* meaning "an enclosed body of water." The term can also be used as a verb—"to collect water"—and often refers to a human-made body of water. Perhaps the question most often asked about the definition is, What's the difference between a pond and a lake? Depends where you live. A 50-acre body of water might be called a pond in Vermont and a lake in Florida. Scientifically, however, limnologists define a pond as a water body of a depth permitting vegetation to grow on the entire bottom, as opposed to a lake where greater depth prevents sunlight from reaching the bottom and stimulating photosynthesis. Ponds are usually standing bodies of water, as opposed to pools, which may form in a river or stream.

Human-made ponds have been used since the beginning of recorded history and are considered by some historians to be humankind's first technology. They were originally built to collect water for convenience and use during drought, household water, agriculture, and livestock water; and later for aquaculture, hydropower, refrigeration ice, fire protection, and to attract wildlife and waterfowl for hunting.

More recently ponds have become popular for recreation and landscaping, as well as wildlife refuges. Recent developments in alternative energy systems have sparked interest in the use of ponds for micro hydro systems and solar and geothermal ponds, as well as making them beneficiaries of new techniques in wind-powered pumping and aeration systems. Global warming is reviving interest in digging ponds for drought relief.

Pond Rotation

Using ponds to raise aquacultural products (fish, waterfowl, and so forth) for a limited amount of time before harvesting the crop, draining the water, and letting the pond lie fallow for a season. Exposing sediment to air allows organic matter to decompose, reducing future oxygen demand. Nuisance aquatic weeds are eradicated and pond sediment can be extracted for use as crop fertilizer. A fallow pond can also be used to grow grain crops for harvest, or perhaps to attract migratory waterfowl. When the pond is refilled it is, in essence, rejuvenated.

See *Drawdown* and *Polyculture.*

Predators

"Shooting fish in a barrel" pretty well describes how easily pond predators can decimate an undefended fish pond. Herons, kingfishers, and otters are some of the worst offenders. Protection includes netting, fencing, scare-away devices (inflatable owl faces, splashers, noisemakers), and lethal traps for unprotected species. Perhaps the ultimate protection: fish cages.

See *Bird Damage Control, Muskrats,* and *River Otters.*

Pumps

Pumps are used in connection with ponds for a variety of purposes: to fill and drain, as well as for irrigation and other agricultural purposes, aeration, circulation, fountains, water gardens, fire protection, dredging, and so on. There are several types of pumps: submersible (electric powered), external (electric, gas, tractor, or wind powered), and hydraulic rams, which run on the energy of falling water. When choosing a pump, determine what it will be used for along with how much water you want to move, and how far. Several pumps are designed specifically for use with waterfalls, fountains, fish ponds, and the like. Oil-free bearings are recommended for submersible pumps to eliminate the potential for contaminating leaks. Efficiency will depend on matching use, pump design, and piping correctly. Saving money on underpowered motors may wind up costing more in electricity used by a straining motor. Choose pipe size to maximize efficiency, because friction loss with undersized pipe decreases efficiency and raises electric costs.

See *Hydraulic Ram*.

Rafts

Ponds used for swimming often feature a floating raft, usually anchored in water deep enough for safe diving. Owners appreciate rafts for their all-around recreational use, and because they are generally accessible to competent swimmers

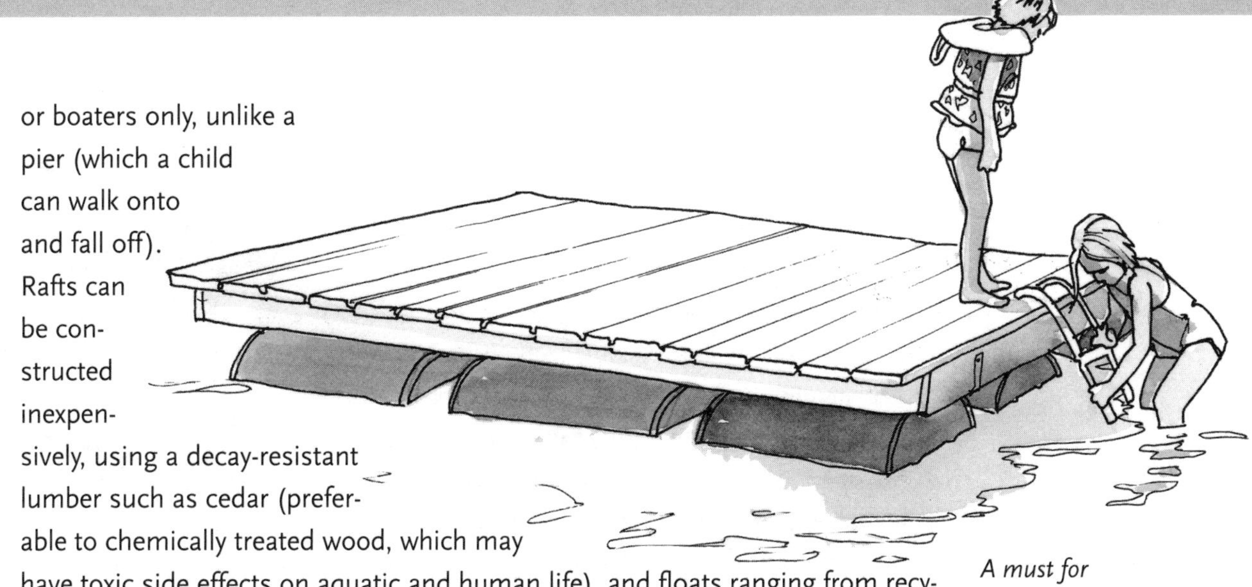

or boaters only, unlike a pier (which a child can walk onto and fall off). Rafts can be constructed inexpensively, using a decay-resistant lumber such as cedar (preferable to chemically treated wood, which may have toxic side effects on aquatic and human life), and floats ranging from recycled barrels to Styrofoam billets, best encased in plastic to protect against animal damage (muskrats like to eat Styrofoam). Rafts make good do-it-yourself projects and are also available from marine suppliers in kit form. Experienced builders recommend a minimum size of 8 feet by 8 feet to prevent instability. Rafts are often anchored and tied to a bolt in the center of the raft, under the planking, with a removable section to simplify mooring. Raft shade creates a cool area for fish in summer. In the North rafts are usually beached during winter to protect them against ice damage and make room for skaters. Floating rafts can also be incorporated into dock systems attached to shore.

A must for recreational ponds, rafts are easy to build, have versatile mooring potential, and are simple to beach in winter to avoid ice damage.

See *Docks and Piers*.

Rakes

Algae and pond weeds can create poor swimming conditions, and pond owners facing aquatic infestation often use manual weed control around beaches. Using various types of rakes can be an effective way to remove aquatic vegetation. Depending on the severity of the problem, useful tools range from common garden rakes to specially designed lake and shore rakes. On a small scale, algae and aquatic weeds can be gathered for removal with a garden rake. Lake and shore rakes feature wider heads with longer teeth, spaced farther apart, to make them more efficient. Some lake rakes with heads a yard or more wide are designed to be pulled behind a boat. These rakes are pulled with chains attached to both ends of the rake head. Rakes can also be used for cutting or uprooting weeds, or gathering previously cut vegetation. Raking is also useful for cleaning up ponds after a drawdown or draining, when the vegetation is dry, lighter, and easy to remove. Lake and shore rakes are available from aquatic supply companies.

Sometimes manual removal of aquatic weeds and alga is the best way to fight nuisance vegetation.

See *Alga* and *Biological Aquatic Pest Management.*

The transition from farm pond to recreational swimming pond has been one of the most significant developments in recent pond design.

Recreational Ponds

Ponds with an emphasis on swimming, skating, and perhaps raising fish. Unlike ponds used for agriculture, fire protection, or other practical uses, recreational ponds emphasize water quality and often feature a sand beach, floating raft, pier, diving board or rock, or what have you. Water may be monitored for coliform bacteria levels to ensure swimmer safety. Recreational ponds are popular with private individuals and rural communities. Public recreational ponds usually require additional safety measures (lifeguard, emergency flotation device, and perhaps fencing, depending on local zoning regulations and insurance requirements). A reliable exchange of fresh water is important, and control of alga and leeches will be appreciated.

Reeds

Emergent wetland plants in the grass family that like marshy areas and ditches. Related to cattails. The tall (5 to 15 feet) varieties (phragmites) produce notable plumelike flower clusters in late summer. Like cattails, they have provided food for Native Americans and habitat and cover for wildlife, as well as purifying polluted water. And like most wetland plants, they may prove invasive in shallow pond areas.

See *Biological Plant Management, Cattails,* and *Invasive Exotic Plants.*

Riprap

See *Crushed Stone.*

River Otters

Often river denizens, but when they plunge into a pond full of fish, watch out: these sleek predators can wipe out a fish crop fast. They also love crawfish. If otters do become a problem, traps may be a successful deterrent. Fish cages, however, offer the ultimate protection.

See *Cage Culture, Fish Ponds,* and *Muskrats.*

Rotenone

A powdered toxin derived from the derris root, used traditionally as a poison for pond owners eliminating an unwanted fish population. (Rotenone is also a popular "natural" garden pesticide.) Rotenone is usually applied in warm weather for maximum effectiveness and relatively quick degradation (cold water use may create long-term toxicity). Most states limit use of rotenone in water to licensed applicators. Because the dosage rate is based on total water volume, ponds are often drawn down before application to reduce the amount used. Rotenone is lethal to various forms of aquatic life, including zooplankton, which may result in increased algal activity.

See *Fish Removal.*

Runoff

The amount of water that drains from a watershed into a pond site or pond. Runoff includes all forms of precipitation, streams and brooks, and snowmelt. Calculating runoff amounts is important when selecting a pond site, and designing the structure and spillway systems.

See *Drainage Field* and *Watershed.*

Sand

A granular material derived from eroded rocks that can be useful in and around ponds. Sand is often used as a beach material, preferably in washed form, which will not cause turbidity due to silt residues. It's used also in sand filtration systems to purify pond water without the use of chemicals and as a general mulching material to suppress aquatic vegetation (it can be spread on ice in winter, to drop later in spring). Sand is also used as a bedding material under plastic and geotextile sheet liners, to insulate against puncturing, and on top as a protective covering. Good stuff, but not recommended for digging a pond in, unless you use a sealant or liner.

See *Beach* and *Sand Filters.*

Sand Filters

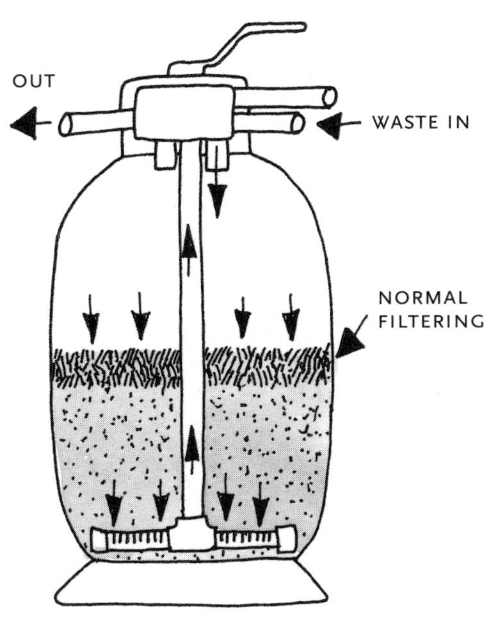

An effective, economical, non-chemical water-quality improvement system.

A simple biological filtration system that uses sand to purify water. Sand filters, often called *slow sand filters,* are being used more and more commonly in wastewater treatment facilities and for drinking water treatment. The advantages include simplicity of setup and operation, relatively low costs, and avoiding chemicals.

Sand filters are also used to help purify water flowing into a pond. Before entering the pond, stream water is run through the sand filter, which helps control algae, bacteria, silt, and sediments including iron, manganese, and phosphorous. Sand filters can also be set up to purify pond water recirculated by pump. Sand filters are effective at removing *Giardia* and other parasites, which makes them useful for public swimming ponds. Eutrophied ponds with algal blooms may respond well to sand filter recirculation.

A simple gravity-flow sand filtration system for a pond usually consists of a filter box filled with a sand of hard durable grain (0.2 to 0.4 millimeter) free from clay, loam, dirt, or organic matter. Between 27 and 30 inches of sand, with an additional 6 to 12 inches that can be removed during cleaning, is usually sufficient. Six to 8 inches of gravel will support the sand and keep it out of the drain system. Gradually a layer of biologically active bacteria builds up on the surface of the sand (the *schmutzdecke*), and it is this layer that does most of the filtration. Running a stream through a sand filter, however, often results in rapid clogging of the system. A silt pool in the stream above the filter may help settle out the undesirable fines. One alternative stream filtration system uses small gravel and large sand in the streambed itself to help avoid clogging. Both systems need periodic cleaning to counteract clogging. Some systems use two filters so one can be cleaned without stopping water treatment.

See *Straw Bale Check Dam.*

Sealants

Used to reduce seepage or leaks in a pond. Unlike plastic, rubber, or geotextile sheet liners, sealants are worked into the soil, applied on top, or added to the water and may not stop seepage completely. Clay and bentonite are natural sealants. Clay is usually packed in a solid layer over porous soil; bentonite is often disked or rototilled into the soil and tamped down. Polymer emulsions can be pumped into a pond, where they settle and reduce leakage. Other sealants include liquid applied-polyurethane mixtures, which do create a leakproof seal. Sealants may be preferable to liners in irregularly shaped ponds, ponds where there is piping to seal around, or where there is concern about puncturing a sheet liner.

See *Gley, Leaks,* and *Liners.*

Secchi Disk

A traditional device for measuring the transparency and nutritional productivity of water. A circular disk with alternating black and white quadrants is lowered into the water, and when it disappears depth is measured. The disappearing point will vary depending on crop and the time of year, as well as the planktonic bloom and general turbidity. For warm-water fish, 12 to 18 inches is considered a good general depth.

See *Turbidity* and *Water Tests.*

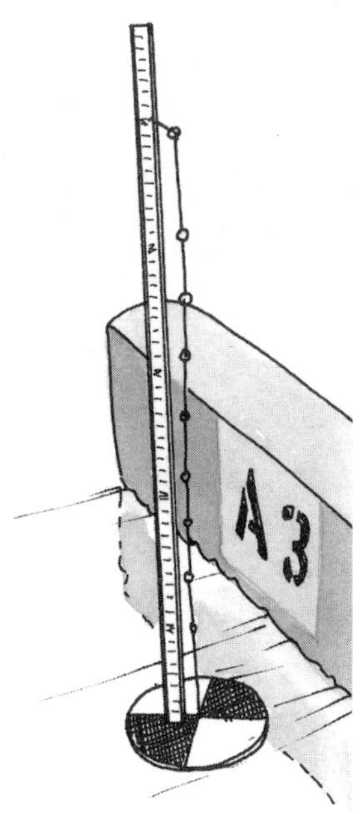

Depending on your intentions, water clouded by alga may be nutritious for some fish, too turbid for others, or unattractive to swimmers. The secchi *disk is a pond owner's dipstick.*

Sedimentation

Over time, sediment accumulates in ponds from watershed inflows and precipitation. The pond is slowly filling and losing depth on its way to becoming a swamp, marsh, or field (eutrophication). Sediment rates are especially affected by erosion, which should be controlled to maximize pond life span. Periodic cleanouts may be necessary to remove sediment.

See *Detention Ponds, Dredging, Eutrophication, Maintenance, Sediment Pools,* and *Straw Bale Check Dams.*

Trapping inflow sediment in upstream pools helps maintain water quality and reduce siltation.

Sediment Pools

One of the most common problems with ponds is siltation. The buildup of silt and sediment is usually due to erosion in the watershed leading to an inflow of suspended solids that settle out and accumulate. Siltation often causes problems with turbidity and loss of depth and storage capacity. Siltation can also involve contamination by pesticides or too much phosphorous, depending on use of the watershed. Siltation is usually a natural process that may not cause a significant problem until changes in watershed use trigger increased erosion. Ponds that depend on a direct inflow of stream water will often experience more problems with siltation than ponds fed by springs, wells, and bypass systems.

One of the best ways to minimize siltation is to construct a silt pool in the feeder stream just above the pond. Sometimes called *detention basins,* these pools help trap sediment before it reaches the pond. Silt pool design depends on the size and velocity of the inflow stream, which in general means the bigger and faster the stream, the bigger the pool. Pools should be at least 1 yard deep, and engineering formulas are available to help match pool size to watershed.* Pools should be designed so they can be periodically cleaned out. Pools are sometimes simply pockets excavated in the streambed, while others may be more elaborate constructions or prefabricated devices such as well tiles or wooden boxes. Builders sometimes use filter fabric or plastic to reinforce silt pools, but they are vulnerable to being undercut by the stream. A series of two or more silt pools is often the most effective sediment trap.

See *Detention Ponds.*

Seines

Nets used to gather fish in tanks and ponds. Sinkers on the bottom edge and floats along the top cause the net to hang vertically, allowing the harvester to pull the ends together and draw the net to shore. Seine mesh is available in

---

* See *Restoration and Management of Lakes and Reservoirs,* by Cooke, Welch, Peterson, and Newroth.

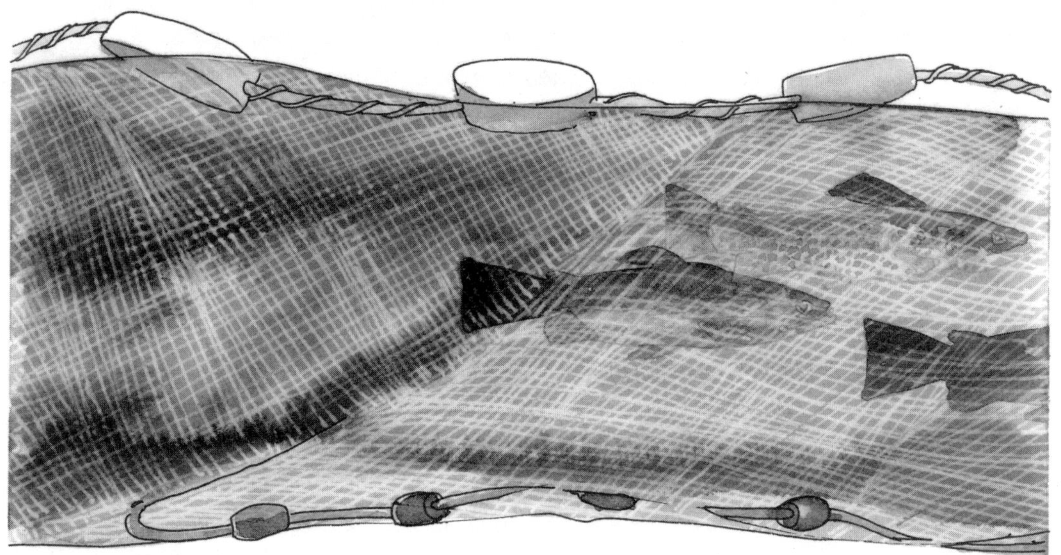

Tossing fish food into the water helps gather fish for seining.

varying sizes, allowing different-size fish to be caught. Rot-resistant nylon netting is usually used, although for catfish it should be treated with a coated material to prevent fish from being snagged in the fibers.

See *Fish Traps* and *Nets.*

Silt Fence

A woven, porous, geotextile fabric fenced across water flows, with its bottom edge tight to the earth (ditched; folded and weighted down with earth or another anchor). It's often used to prevent silt from entering a pond from an eroding inflow stream or to prevent silt from flowing downstream from a pond-construction site. It may be mandatory at pond-construction sites to protect the downstream watershed from turbid water. Coils of excelsior or other natural filtering material can also be used.

See *Straw Bale Check Dams.*

Siphons

On sloping terrain siphon hoses or piping can be used for gravity flow of water for crops, livestock, and other needs. A garden hose with a shut-off valve or nozzle may be all that's needed. Flexible PVC can be used for more permanent installations. Siphons can also be used as overflow systems. Flexible piping enables the pond owner to direct overflow where it may be useful. Depending on the terrain, siphons can be set up so that the intake is near the bottom of the pond. Unlike a standpipe or earth-cut spillway, which takes water off the top of the pond, a submerged siphon picks up deep water, which is lower in dissolved oxygen. This may be an advantage for fish growers who want to maintain high oxygen levels, especially in summer.

See *Spillways.*

Site Surveys

Pond designs may benefit from site surveys to map the topography. These are usually done by an engineer, surveyor, or pond designer. Depending on state and federal laws and the size of the pond, topographic surveys and plans by a licensed engineer may be necessary to get a building permit.

Site surveys are usually shot with a transit and leveling rod. A profile of the centerline of the dam is used to determine the height of the embankment; profiles of the centerline of the main spillway and auxiliary emergency spillway are used to determine location and slopes. Surveys also can enable the designer/contractor to calculate the amount of material needed to build the embankment, the volume of water in the finished pond, and cost.

See *Maps* and *Transit.*

Sky Ponds

A traditional term for natural ponds that depend on rainfall and other precipitation for filling. Sky ponds tend to be located in low-lying terrain, and the water level will vary depending on precipitation.

See *Vernal Pools.*

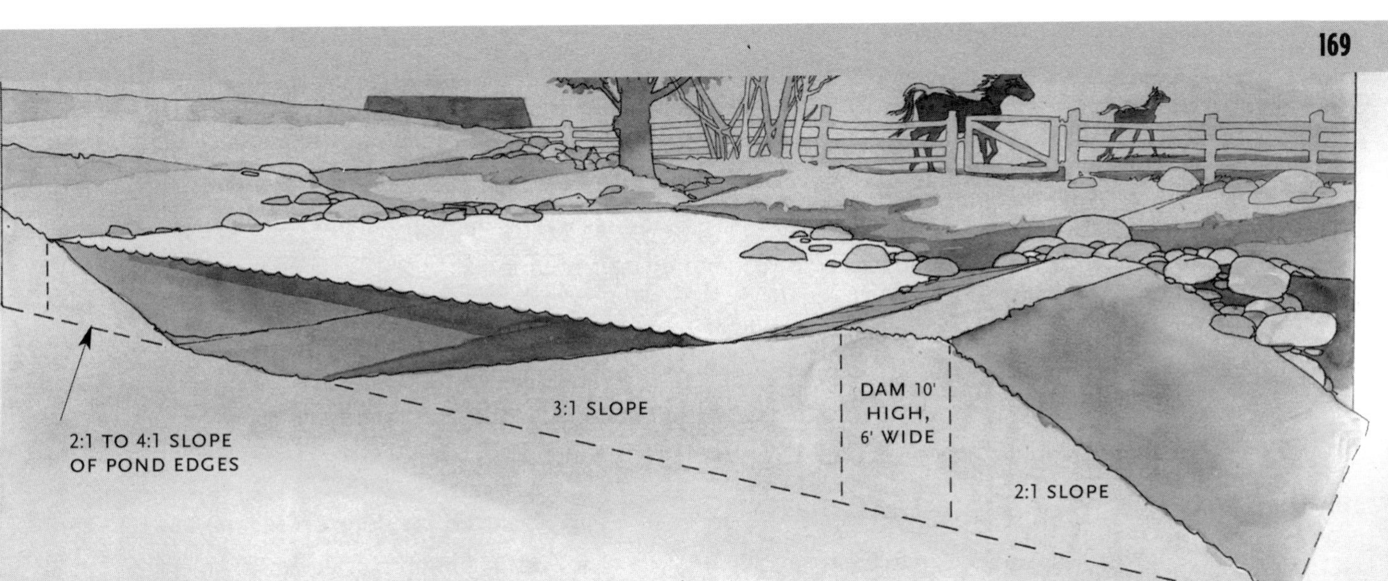

Slope

Interior and exterior pond slope angles will affect water volume, structural durability, aquatic vegetation, and embankment maintenance.

The angle of grade of the terrain in a pond basin, embankment, overflow channel, and watershed. Expressed in degrees or as a ratio between fall and distance (3 to 1 means a vertical drop of 1 foot for every 3 horizontal feet; 1 to 1 is a 45-degree angle). Slope plays a significant role in pond design and management. In an excavated pond, recommended basin slopes range between 2 to 1 and 4 to 1 or even flatter. Steep slopes tend to slump and should not be used if the material is excessively silty. Three to one is a generally durable basin slope.

Basin slopes affect water quality. Steeper slopes tend to discourage aquatic vegetation. Shallow slopes foster warm sunny water, which encourages vegetation and algae. Still, pond owners may wish to avoid steep slopes as a safety precaution if children play around the pond. Flatter slopes are also used in beach areas.

Slope is a consideration in ponds with fluctuating water levels—for instance, irrigation ponds. The more basin slope that's exposed as water levels drop, the more the exposure to possible erosion (as well as generally unattractive appearance). Steep slopes also yield more water volume.

Slope is an important design element in embankment construction. Again, 3 to 1 is a commonly accepted slope for the outside face of a dam. Two to one is possible with well-compacted, good soil material, but keep in mind that steep slopes may be difficult to keep mowed.

Slope is a factor in earth-cut spillway design. The overflow slope should not be steep enough to cause erosion or direct runoff down an unprotected embankment where erosion is a possibility. Inlet stream slopes should not be steep enough to cause erosion and siltation or so flat that water doesn't drain into the pond.

On hilly terrain a watershed drainage area with excessively steep slopes may encourage erosion, and stabilizing measures should be taken (reinforcements, drainage, grade alteration). Basin and embankment slopes in the same pond can vary according to structural and landscaping requirements.

In some ponds where water demands require large volume, or natural slopes won't hold, some or all of the structure may need reinforcement with vertical retaining walls (stone, concrete reinforcing block, or the like).

See *Embankment.*

Sluice Gate

In the past sluice gates were associated with millponds utilizing sluiceways to deliver water to a waterwheel; the term can also refer to water control structures used to regulate water levels in a pond. Depending on construction technique, it may also be called a *stoplog* or *splashboard control structure*. Generally, a sluice gate is a concrete gate located at the pond outflow. The gate consists of wing walls on the upstream sides of the overflow channel, and sometimes on down-stream sides. Water flows through a passage between the wing walls, based on a concrete foundation constructed deep enough to prevent undermining and leakage. Control of the overflow is obtained by installing stoplogs or splash-boards in slots in the walls. Sluice gates for millponds often used steel doors that could be raised or lowered by mechanical means; water flowed through the bottom of the gate. The pond water level is manipulated according to the amount of logs or splashboards used, and water flows over the top of the gate. The width of the gate is usually no more than 4 or 5 feet because water pressure would otherwise bend the boards. Steel rods are sometimes installed in the boards to use as handles or fittings to aid in removal. Caulking, tongue-and-groove fittings, or even plastic sheeting may help prevent leakage between the boards.

Unlike most water-level outlet pipe spillways, which can be fitted with valves to control overflow volume, gates are used to manipulate water levels. Water-level control is useful in wetland management where draining and flooding can be used to stimulate aquatic growth in shallow water and then create deeper areas for waterfowl feeding and overwintering. Water-level control is also useful for maintaining high levels in summer and preventing flooding in winter and spring. Opening the sluice gate is also a convenient way to flush out sediment. Sluice gates are especially effective in manipulating water levels in low-flow ponds; care should be taken in large-volume ponds, where unloading water can be dangerous to downstream areas.

See *Water Control Structures.*

Snails

Native to many North American freshwater ponds and lakes, snails can play a significant role in the food chain—cleaning up algae and dead plant and animal matter and providing food in turn for fish and other animals. Varieties include the trapdoor, black ramshorn, and pond snail. Water gardeners and aquarium owners often stock snails because their scavenging activities help maintain an ecologically balanced habitat (sometimes without the need for chemicals or mechanical filtration). Certain varieties of snails will devour valuable water garden plants, however, and can contribute to swimmer's itch (schistosome dermatitis). The flukes that cause swimmer's itch are released by snails during warm weather and may penetrate human skin, causing skin irritation. If I were using a pond for swimming, I'd think twice before stocking snails.

See *Crawfish* and *Biological Aquatic Plant Management.*

Sod

Grassy turf grown and harvested for landscaping. Prohibitions against using fertilizer around ponds (to protect water quality) and soil compaction after construction can make growing grass from seed difficult. Sod can be used to create a quick grass cover for erosion prevention and landscaping.

Soft Water

Often found on bedrock and other rock types with low buffering capacity; susceptible to changes in the acidity of waters that affect it. Appreciated by homeowners because it's low in substances such as calcium and magnesium salts that prevent lathering of soap, but in ponds it may not be productive of aquatic life because of its low alkalinity.

See *Alkalinity* and *Hard Water.*

Soil Tests

Unless you're going to depend on a liner or sealant, good soil is required for a successful pond. A clay content of between 10 and 20 percent is generally rec-

Determining clay content in pond soil is an essential step in site selection.

ommended. Soil in a potential pond site can be tested for clay content by placing a sample in a jar, adding water, and shaking it up. When it clears, the clay will have settled last, and the proportion can be measured against the silt, gravel, and so on. More elaborate soil texture kits are available from aquaculture supply outfits and technical instrument suppliers. Soil can be tested for pH, too, to determine the effect of acidity or alkalinity on the future pond.

Soil tests can also be used to determine moisture content and compaction. Moisture content and compaction are usually tested for by engineers during the preparation and construction of a dam. Soil that's too wet or dry doesn't compact properly, and dams are usually built in "lifts," or layers, which must be properly packed.

See *Clay* and *Test Pits.*

Solar Ponds

Ponds can be used to trap solar radiation for heating and other forms of energy generation. A solar pond, also known as a *salt gradiant pond,* contains a layer of saline water at the bottom, which traps heat and prevents it from rising. A dark-colored liner on the bottom will increase absorption of solar radiation as well as provide a protective membrane (pollution of surrounding land can be a concern if the pond is not lined). Water temperatures in the lower layer can reach close to the boiling point. Heat is tapped as hot water, or used to generate hot air, for industrial processes including salt production, desalinization, aquaculture, dairy farming, and food processing. It can also be used to heat recreational swimming pools.

Solar ponds are most efficient in warm climates where salt or saline water is readily available, and fossil fuels or other forms of energy are scarce. Israel is a pioneer in the use of solar ponds, and they are also found in Australia and India. Solar ponds are not used extensively in the United States.

See *Geothermal Ponds.*

Spillways

Any of various pond overflow systems, including native spillway (earth-cut channel), T-riser, drop inlet, hood inlet (generally referred to as *trickle tubes*), stoplog gates and boxes, and sluice gates.

See *Drop Inlet, Emergency Spillway, Hood Inlet, T-Riser,* and *Water Control Structures.*

This splitter combined with a trash rack screens out debris and prevents erosion.

Splitter

See *Anti-Vortex Device.*

Stagnant Water

When water stops flowing in and out of a pond for any length of time, the water becomes stagnant. Stagnant water leads to higher temperatures, greater oxygen demands, algal blooms, possible fish-kills and mosquitoes. If the situation is allowed to continue, a stagnant pond will be vulnerable to colonization by aquatic weeds and algae: eutrophication. It's not unusual for a pond to become briefly stagnant during the height of dry summer weather. This may lead to problems with fish-kills if the pond is heavily stocked, shallow, and not equipped with backup aeration or supplementary fresh water. Fortunately, many ponds experience only brief periods of summer stagnation, and fall/winter rains restore a freshwater exchange. Remedies for stagnation include aeration, supplementary water, recirculation of existing water, and leak repairs.

See *Eutrophication.*

Standpipe

See *T-Riser.*

Stonework

Long considered one of the key elements in pond design. The Chinese mastered pond construction more than 2,000 years ago and used the solid, stable nature of natural, uncut stone as an aesthetic counterbalance to water's fluidity. Stones were used ornamentally and for paths, walls, terraces, waterfalls, stepping-stones, and islands. The Chinese also believed that certain stones possessed supernatural powers.

Today stones are used for practical and aesthetic purposes both in and around ponds. Pond construction often benefits from a variety of stonework. Stones can help stabilize and guide inflows and spillways. Stone can be used to build reinforcing walls in unstable shore areas or to create a vertical wall inside the structure for stability and/or increased water volume. Stone can be used as a

In wet shoreline areas, a retaining wall prevents erosion and slumping and enhances the pond's aesthetic appeal.

foundation for piers, docks, and bridges or as a bridge span itself. Stone can be used as an edging material to prevent shore erosion, especially in ponds vulnerable to strong winds. Lining submerged edge areas with stone can discourage unwanted aquatic vegetation, as well as muskrats. Piles of stone at the pond bottom provide habitat for fish. Stone can be used to create an island, an especially popular feature in water gardens. Stone is a good material for creating paths around a pond, and stepping-stones can be laid in the water itself.

Stone is also appreciated as a landscaping element in waterfalls leading in and out of the pond, terraces, benches, diving rocks, and for ornamental effects.

Straw

A traditional remedy for pond turbidity. Straw is placed in shallow edge areas around the pond; as it decomposes, turbidity is reduced. Old hay is recommended. As the straw decomposes, it releases positively charged particles that join with negatively charged clay particles, allowing clay to settle. Barley straw is used by some water gardeners and pond owners to control filamentatious algae. Straw has also been used to cover and suppress odors in wastewater treatment ponds.

See *Barley Straw* and *Gypsum.*

Straw Bale Check Dams

Erosion around new ponds, and in upstream watersheds, can be counteracted by installing straw bales to filter sediment.

Used to prevent soil erosion around a construction area or stop erosion in waterways, straw bale check dams are also employed extensively around pond-construction sites, especially to prevent sediment from damaging downstream fishing habitats and degrading water quality, and to control inflow areas.

Straw bale check dams are usually staked down in overflow and inflow channels around the pond site to filter water and prevent erosion. Geotextile mesh fabrics are sometimes used to reinforce the upstream face of the bale dam. Bale dams or other silt barriers are often mandated by environmental agencies that regulate pond construction.

Unfortunately, bale check dams can cause as much or more trouble than they're designed to prevent. If they're not properly installed, which is often the case, water can undercut the structure or flow around it, causing erosion; the bales can wash downstream, plugging culverts. If they do function properly during a construction period, they're often left behind afterward, unmaintained, eventually causing damage. Waterlogged straw bale barriers are difficult to move, which is often the reason they're left behind. Abandoned bale check dams faced with fabric mesh look like industrial litter.

Bale check dams work best in relatively flat areas and should be used for a short time during pond construction, then removed.

See *Filters* and *Sediment Pools.*

Stream Ponds

Streams have long been a traditional source of pond water, and indeed until not long ago, many ponds were dug in the direct path of a watercourse. Convenient to be sure, but not without problems. Sediment flowing into the pond often accelerated eutrophication, and before long the pond might wind up a shallow swamp. Some stream pond builders installed spillway gates that could be opened periodically to release water and flush out silt. Still, state and federal environmental agencies began to object to stream ponds, which interrupt the migration of fish, threaten downstream areas with occasional floods of sediment, cheat downstream areas of water needed for aquifer recharge, and dry up the stream itself. In most areas of the country, pond building in year-round streams is now prohibited.

There are, however, ways to build a stream pond that will not interrupt fish migration and the free flow of water. In fact, these "digger ponds" are often highly oxygenated pools favorable to fish health.

See *Digger Ponds, Sluice Gate,* and *Water Control Structures.*

Swale

A depression cut in the earth to control water flow. It can be used in the watershed above a pond to help direct runoff into or around a pond or below the pond to guide overflow.

See *Berm*.

Swimmer's Itch

See *Snails* and *Waterborne Illness*.

Swivel Pipe

A drop-inlet overflow standpipe that pivots at the elbow and allows the pipe to rotate up and down, making it possible to raise and lower a pond's water level. Unlike most fixed standpipes, which only affect the volume of overflow, a swivel pipe gives you control over the pond water level. Sometimes it can be helpful to raise the overflow level in summer to store water for dry periods and lower the inlet in winter and spring to prevent flooding. Swivel pipes can also be used to manipulate water levels in wildlife wetlands, where shallow water in summer encourages vegetative growth and high water in fall and winter supports migrating waterfowl. Swivel pipes may be vulnerable to ice and wave action damage because the standpipe is not stabilized by surrounding fill.

See *Sluice Gate* and *Water Control Structures.*

Test Pits

Pond building begins with site evaluation, and there's nothing more essential to site analysis than test pits. Borings in the soil will reveal information about soil quality, groundwater, and possible obstructions by ledge rock. A landowner may prefer to begin checking out pond sites manually, with a hand auger, saving the expense of hiring a backhoe. Hand augers are especially practical in sites inaccessible to a backhoe without road work or clearing. There's no point in tearing up the landscape and then finding out the site's no good. Still, most contractors prefer to excavate with a machine.

The pond site should not include underground electrical lines, water pipes, or other obstacles. It's important to dig at least 8 feet deep in at least two or three locations, because soil quality may vary throughout the site. The borings are usually narrow and deep, and they may be refilled after the site is examined or left to be monitored for changes in the water table. Ideally, test pits should be dug during dry summer weather to determine worst-case-scenario water levels, especially if the pond will depend on groundwater alone. If the test pits are not refilled soon after excavation, care should be taken to make sure excavated material is piled up far enough from the hole to ensure it doesn't erode back into the test pit or cause the hole to slump. Open test pits are often covered with plywood or some kind of protective lid to prevent accidents to people or animals.

Soil excavated from the test pit should be examined to determine clay content. Soil with good water-retaining clay should be sticky and hold together in a ball when compressed. Sandy, "dirty" material is not encouraging. Neither is ledge rock. Although ledge is often found near springs and underground water, it is also usually fissured and leak, and has been the downfall of many ponds.

A promising test pit may fill with water quickly, or overnight. If the water level is well below the surface, it indicates a poor pond site, unless supplementary water is available. I've seen test pits that hit an underground stream at 8 feet, but the water was gushing through a streak of sand. The boring was refilled and the pond plan abandoned.

Excavated ponds on flat terrain often depend on groundwater; test pits in those sites are, in effect, miniature versions of the pond-to-be. Naturally, the more water, the better the chance for success. Test pits for embankment ponds, designed to capture watershed runoff and streams, may be examined more for soil quality and ledge. Test pits should not be neglected in the embankment area, where good material and a solid foundation are essential to success.

See *Auger* and *Soil Tests*.

Transit

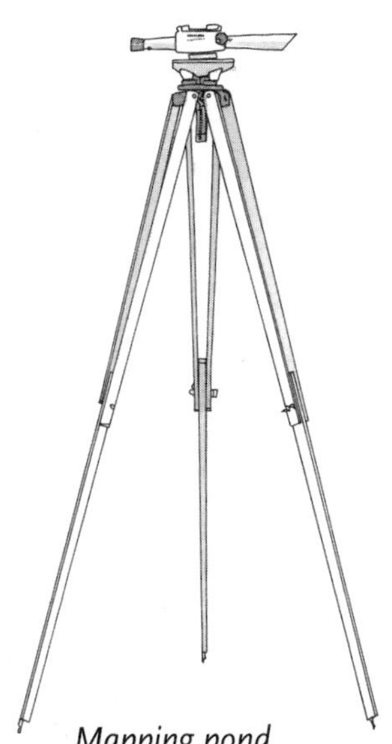

Mapping pond site contours and building a level dam requires this basic engineering tool.

A surveying instrument used with a leveling rod for construction and property mapping; it's also used by engineers for pond site surveys to determine topography and elevations, especially in the mapping and design of embankments and spillways. Until recently, transits featured a telescope and level on a tripod; lately, lasers have also been incorporated for greater measuring accuracy. Transits are also used by pond contractors to shoot levels for accurate finish grading of embankments. Small telescopic hand levels can be used for rough estimates of elevations when choosing a pond site and to estimate embankment height.

See *Site Surveys.*

Trash Guard

Pipe spillways may be vulnerable to becoming clogged with floating debris and trash. Depending on the type of spillway, diameter, and pond litter, a trash guard may be necessary. In general, the smaller the pipe diameter, the more likely it will be to clog. (The USDA recommends against spillway pipe smaller than 6 inches.) Trash guards are manufactured by pipe suppliers to fit various-sized inlets. They include flat steel-mesh grates, bar guards, strainers, and perforated rigid tubing. The problem with trash guards is that they can become clogged themselves unless periodically monitored and cleaned. In fact, many pond owners prefer not to use trash guards at all. Bar guards are generally preferable to smaller mesh screens because they tend not to clog. Contractors and pond owners may prefer to build their own trash racks, using widely spaced iron rods and angle iron or wooden posts to box off the inlet. Large trash racks are also more effective against beavers. Pipe spillways may also have to be protected at the outlet end against rats and other rodents.

This hardware will put your beavers on a tree-free diet.

Ponds with high-volume overflow may benefit from incorporating an anti-vortex baffle plate, or splitter, with the trash guard. This prevents whirlpooling, which can cause erosion around the pipe. Anti-vortex baffles may also be installed as a precaution against 100-year-frequency storm discharge.

See *Anti-Vortex Device* and *Beaver Baffles.*

Tree Wrap

Flexible wire mesh used to protect trees from beavers, which might otherwise fell them for food and dam building. Tree wrap is used around ponds and in wetland areas. It should protect the tree at least 4 feet above the ground, including the potential snow level.

See *Beavers* and *Beaver Repellents.*

Trickle Tube

See *Drop Inlet*, *Hood Inlet*, and *T-Riser*.

T-Riser

A vertical pipe connected to the overflow and drain; used to control a pond's water level and prevent spillway erosion. The riser and drain overflow resemble an inverted T. The riser opening is set at the desired pond water level, and after that level is reached, surplus water overflows through the system. A gate or valve on the drain can be opened to drain the pond.

T-risers are usually installed in embankment ponds, with the horizontal overflow pipe buried below frost level. The riser diameter is calculated according to the size of the watershed draining into the pond and regional flood rainfall estimates. Pipe extensions are sometimes added or removed to change the water level. The traditional pipe material was iron or steel; sewer-grade plastic is often used today. PVC outlet control box structures with variable gate openings are also available.

To reduce seepage, anti-seep collars should be installed on the riser and horizontal pipes. To discourage clogging with debris or by rodents, the riser should be at least 6 inches in diameter. Trash racks are sometimes installed to prevent clogging, and anti-vortex splitters to prevent erosion.

See *Drain*, *Drop Inlet*, *Embankment*, *Hood Inlet*, *Spillway*, *Standpipe*, and *Water Control Structures*.

Turbidity

Cloudy, opaque water characteristic of unsettled soil and/or algal blooms. *Turbid water* usually refers to water muddied by sediment stirred up by erosion, or rainfall, or even an electrical charge in some clay particles that prevents them from precipitating. Depending on what soils are involved, turbid water can look red, gray, or coffee brown; in the case of algal blooms, the water will be green. Turbid water isn't particularly attractive, especially to swimmers, and by cutting off sunlight the turbidity reduces healthy plant and fish growth. It may also be a sign of siltation, leading to sediment buildup on the pond bed, or eutrophication, indicating poor oxygen levels and plant colonization.

Remedies for turbid water begin with an analysis of the cause. If the cloudy water occurs after a rainfall, it may be due to soil eroding into the pond. A good grass cover around the pond shore can often cut turbidity dramatically. Sometimes a filter or sediment pool in the inflow channel may be required. Inflow channels and the surrounding watershed should be protected from erosion. Turbid water may also be caused by bottom-feeding fish such as carp or by crawfish.

If the turbidity is due to unsettled clay particles, one traditional remedy is to scatter hay around the edge of the pond; the slightly acidic effect of submersion or rainfall runoff helps clarify the water. Green grass clippings are even more effective.

Mineral additives can also help precipitate soil particles. Agricultural gypsum, limestone, aluminum sulfate, and fertilizers are all used to clarify pond water.

Natural biological elements such as bacterial nitrofers can also be used. If the problem is due to algal blooms, remedies may be found in biological controls, aeration, improvement of the nitrogen to phosphorous ratio, and enhancement of zooplankton.

Newly constructed ponds are usually turbid after they fill and take time to settle out. Silty clays that tend to cause turbidity are sometimes track-packed during pond construction and covered with crushed stone and/or filter fabric to suppress cloudy water. Herbicides that kill algal blooms may cure turbid water temporarily, but the problem usually recurs. Toxic chemicals should be considered as a last resort, if at all.

See *Gypsum* and *Straw*.

U.S. Army Corps of Engineers (USACE)

The branch of the U.S. Army with authority over many aspects of water resources (flood control, environmental protection, and so on), including pond construction on private land where protected wetlands and/or dams may be involved. Since 1972 the USACE has been responsible for enforcing the wetlands regulations of the Clean Water Act. Wetland pond construction of more than 3,000 square feet may require Corps permission. In some states, pond dams over a certain height also require Corps permission and may need engineering plans.

See *Permitting*.

Vegetation

A pond has the potential to be a liquid garden, although most owners of large ponds generally prefer to keep the vegetation to a minimum (water gardens and wetlands excepted). There are three types of pond vegetation: submergent, floating leaved, and emergent. Submergent plants are rooted in the pond bed and grow underwater. Floating-leaved plants are rooted in the pond bed and have at least some leaves floating on the water. Emergent plants are rooted in the pond bed and rise above the pond's surface. Widely dispersed submergent plants include many kinds of pondweed, several species of water milfoil, coontail, bladderwort, and muskgrass. Common floating-leaved plants include duckweed, water lily, and smartweed. Emergent plants include arrowhead, pickerelweed, cattail, and reed grass. Most pond plants have the potential to colonize water bodies, especially in shallow, stagnant, high-nutrient conditions. Pond owners usually take precautions to restrict plants to small areas (a stand of cattails is attractive and offers food and cover for birds, for example). Otherwise, shore edges and overall depths are maintained to discourage plants. Some pond owners do like the visual effect of aquatic vegetation, as well as its contribution of habitat and cover for birds and animals. Care should be taken, however, to make sure that plants don't take over the pond completely, with negative effects on fish and water quality.

See *Biological Aquatic Plant Management* and *Invasive Exotic Plants.*

Vent

An air relief pipe that may be installed at various points along the waterline feeding the pond, hydropower unit, or the like. It prevents bubbles from air locking the flow by allowing the pipe to "burp." It's often used in gravity-flow systems.

See *Gravity Feed.*

Vernal Pools

Temporary pools that collect water in spring from snowmelt and precipitation and create a breeding habitat for frogs, salamanders, and other aquatic life (mosquitoes and blackflies included). Vernal pools play an important part in the ecosystem and usually dry up during summer. They sometimes make a promising site for pond construction, although they may be considered protected wetland habitat or require permitting.

See *Sky Ponds.*

Wastewater Treatment Ponds

Ponds are used for wastewater treatment in a number of different ways. Some use natural oxidation and plant photosynthesis (algae) to improve water quality. More sophisticated systems add aeration devices to improve the natural decomposition of organic pollutants. Anaerobic ponds are used as sediment traps for treatment of industrial and agricultural wastes. All wastewater management systems rely on gravity to settle sediment, as well as on natural biological processes. Because photosynthesis is enhanced in shallow water, depth is an important design criterion. Treatment ponds are usually lined with a protective membrane to prevent groundwater contamination.

By providing a natural means of improving wastewater quality, these ponds save money and reduce the need for chemical treatment. Many ponds are used as pretreatment systems that remove substantial contaminants before the water is "polished" by filtration and/or chemicals and released back to groundwater or municipal water systems. Some wastewater ponds are designed to retain liquids until they evaporate. Constructed wetlands are also used for natural wastewater treatment.

The potential for disease and odor problems requires pond managers to monitor and control water quality, mosquitoes, wildlife, and so forth.

See *Constructed Wetlands* and *Detention Ponds.*

Waterborne Illness

Swimming ponds can host bacteria and other pathogens capable of causing illness. Swimming in contaminated water may result in skin rashes, sore throats, earaches, diarrhea, or more serious problems. Children are more likely to swallow water when swimming and become ill if the water is contaminated. Infants, the elderly, and people with weakened immune systems may become seriously ill.

The *E. coli* bacterium is one of the most common sources of illness. It is usually associated with human or animal feces and is commonly tested for in public recreational waters. Test kits are also sold for private analysis, and private labs and state health departments offer testing.

Giardiasis is a gastrointestinal illness caused by a parasite transmitted by animal or human feces. It is often associated with beaver-populated waters. Water tests for the *Giardia* pathogen require an elaborate sampling procedure and expensive fee—and may not be accurate. Unfortunately, it is not usually detected until present in the host.

Swimmer's itch is a skin rash caused by an allergic reaction to infection with certain parasites of birds and animals. It is commonly caused by birds or mammals depositing infected feces in a pond, where eggs are transmitted to aquatic snails, which produce the larvae that cause the problem. Toweling off after swimming helps prevent infection.

Other sources of waterborne illness include certain varieties of blue-green algae, the *Cryptosporidium* parasite, and viruses. Chlorine is sometimes used to disinfect ponds, but it also kills beneficial aquatic life, and unless used regularly has a limited effectiveness. Filtration can also help remove certain pathogens. Keeping the pond and watershed as free of fecal waste products as practical is probably the best strategy. Mosquito control is essential to preventing the spread of the West Nile virus.

See *Biological Insect Pest Control, Mosquitoes, Sand Filters,* and *Snails.*

Water Circulators

Pumps or water movement systems can be used to circulate water to improve water quality. Recirculating pumps are frequently used in water gardens, often combined with a water filter. Water may be pumped back into water gardens (and sometimes ponds) down a constructed waterfall, as a landscape feature and aerator. In ponds and water gardens, water may also be pumped out and sprayed back in via fountains as a means of aeration. Circulation helps destratify water, which improves oxygen levels and discourages algae in the top layer of water. Pumps can also be used in ponds to move water out of an aquifer beneath a sheet or clay liner and back into the pond. Both submersible and external pumps are used for water circulation. The advantage of submersible pumps is silence; they do need to be installed with anticlogging devices, however, which may require periodic cleaning. External pumps are easier to maintain, but in areas that freeze they may need to be disconnected and drained in winter.

Floating water circulators that use submerged propeller-like devices to move water are also used in ponds to improve water quality and enhance fish growth. These circulators hang in the water under floats, and can be height adjusted. External electric power lines are required, as they are for submersible pumps.

See *Aeration* and *Pumps*.

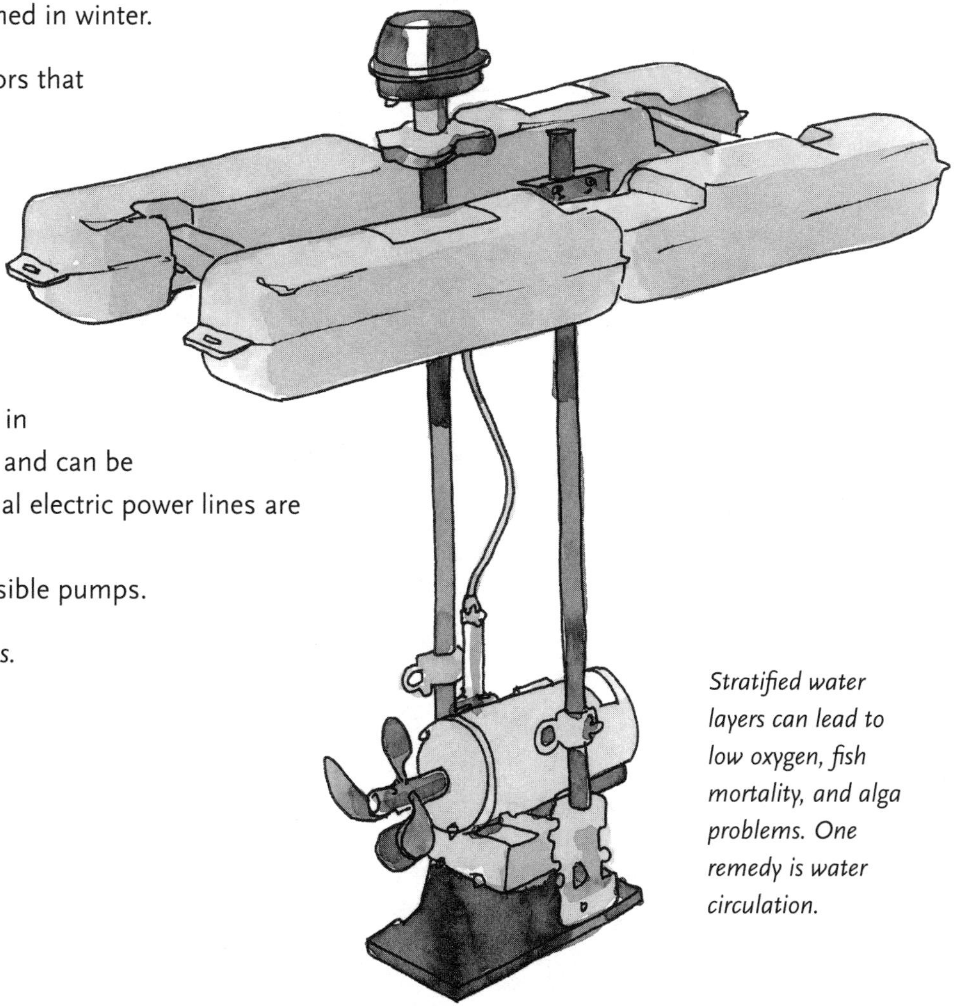

Stratified water layers can lead to low oxygen, fish mortality, and alga problems. One remedy is water circulation.

Water Conditioners

Additives used to improve water quality for fish culture, algal control, water clarity, pH levels, recreational use, and more. Conditioners range from natural products such as beneficial bacteria, salts, and calcium to chemical herbicides, fungicides, and bacterial controls. In some cases, permits may be required to use water conditioners in ponds.

See *Bacteria.*

Water Control Structures

What goes in must come out, and in the case of constructed ponds and wetlands, overflow can discharge through earth-cut spillways, pipes, or—for more precise water management—water control structures. Water control structures are designed and built to allow the pond manager to raise or lower water levels in small increments, often to enhance waterfowl habitat. They should be constructed as high as the maximum desired water level, as well as designed to allow for complete drainage.

Water control structures can be as simple as a standpipe with removable pipe sections; standpipes can also be designed to swivel, so the inlet can be dropped to lower the water level. Agri Drain Corporation offers a control box with

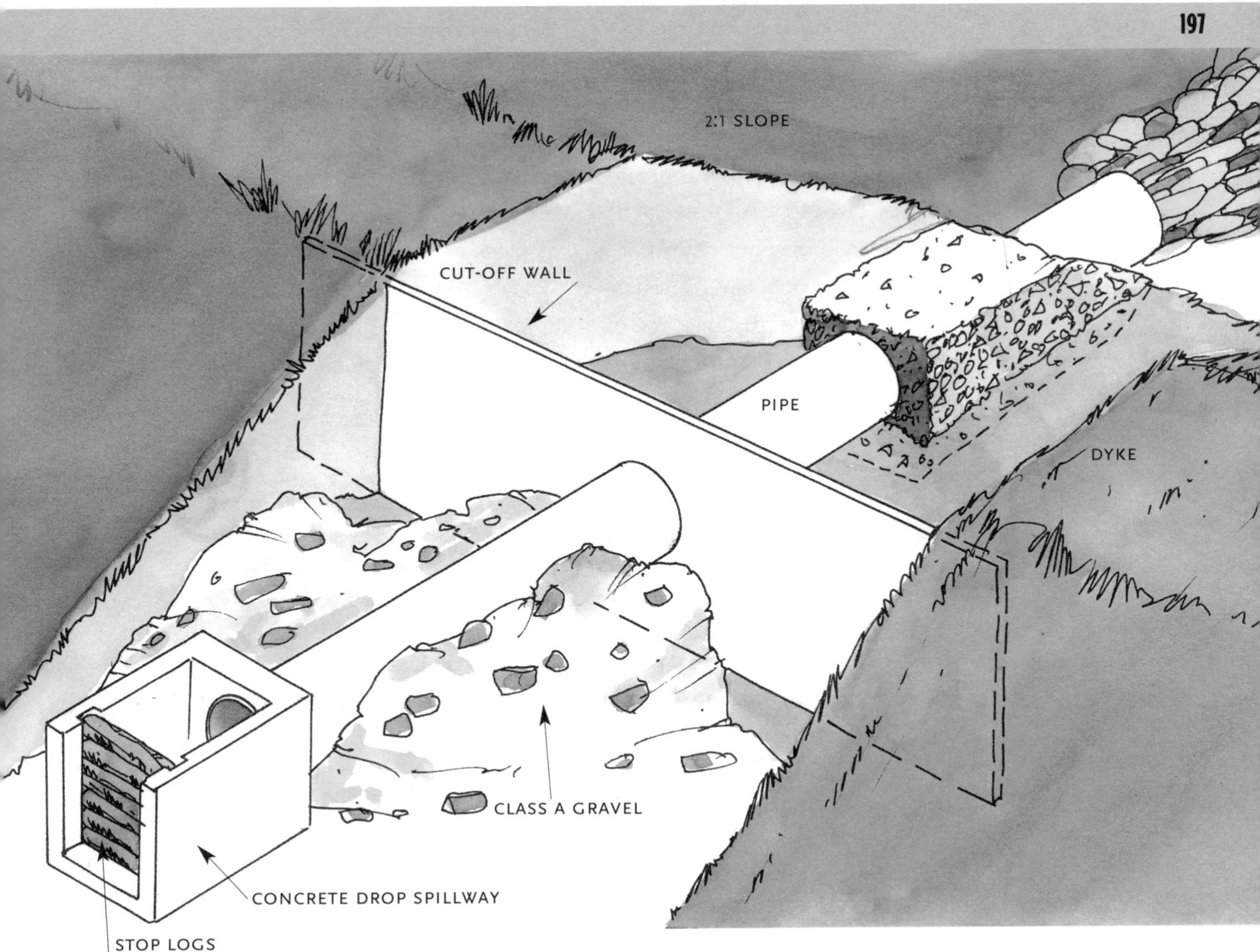

Manipulating water levels allows pond managers to prevent flood damage, reserve water during dry spells, and drain and flood ponds to attract waterfowl.

adjustable panels to allow accurate water-level control. Probably the most familiar control structure is the stoplog type, recommended by the U.S. Fish and Wildlife Service. This is a concrete box about 4 feet wide by 3 feet deep and as tall as it takes to accommodate both complete drainage and maximum water level. Slots in the front of the box hold stoplogs or boards, which are installed or removed to manipulate the water level. Redwood or other rot-resistant lumber is recommended for the logs, and caulking (or tongue-and-groove) may be needed to waterproof the seams between the logs.

See *Moist-Soil Management*, *Sluice Gate*, and *Swivel Pipe*.

Waterfall

A stream of water cascading into a pond can add aesthetic and practical benefits. Visually, a waterfall can play a significant role in pond landscaping, dramatizing a water source and bringing attention to attractive stonework, as well as contributing a pleasing sound. Water splashing into a pond also has an aerating effect, adding dissolved oxygen to the water, which can be a plus for fish and water quality. In summer, recirculated waterfalls may increase water temperature.

A stream flowing into a pond will usually erode the streambed, entering the pond near its water level. It takes a large elevated slab of stone or ledge at the inlet to create a waterfall, and if not present naturally, the waterfall designer must create it. Stonework at the inlet area is built up and capped with one or more stones that the stream flows over before splashing into the pond. Waterfall stones should be wide enough so that the stream doesn't cut around the edges and deep enough to prevent undercutting. Stones are often slightly depressed in the middle to funnel water down the middle. The outlet stone is often set with an overlapping forward edge to create the waterfall drop. Additional stones behind and beside the waterfall can create an echo-chamber effect to increase the sound.

It's important to remember that running a stream directly into a pond may cause sediment accumulation. To avoid this, waterfalls may be constructed using gravity-feed pipes from an upstream source, pump and pipe systems feeding from an external source, or recirculation of the pond water.

See *Water Gardens.*

Waterfowl

The arrival of geese, ducks, and other migratory waterfowl may be a blessing or a curse, depending on a pond owner's point of view. Wild waterfowl are naturally attracted to ponds, especially those offering food (everything from well-manicured grass to native plants), protective cover (high grasses and shrubs), and secure refuge (islands). They may select a pond as a temporary layover during migration, for longer periods of nesting and raising their young, or for winter shelter. Some owners welcome waterfowl, enjoying the spectacle of wild birds and glad to provide them a refuge; hunters may maintain ponds to provide refuge as well as attract game for bird season.

Pond owners who wish to attract waterfowl may plant grains and grasses favored by geese and ducks and build nesting platforms and islands. Owners are often pleased to find that waterfowl have a voracious appetite for algae and aquatic plants and do a good job of weed control. Waterfowl are also raised as a crop (meat, eggs, feathers, live birds), in which case the pond is usually outfitted with nesting houses and fenced off.

The ability of geese and ducks to curtail algae leads some pond owners to stock domestic waterfowl to control unwanted vegetation. They may raise them simply for aesthetic reasons. But if the pond is also used for recreation, this can backfire. Geese, especially, can turn out to be a serious nuisance, littering the shore with waste matter, contaminating the water, and even attacking people. Wild geese landing at a recreational pond may cause the same problems if allowed to establish themselves.

See *Bird Damage Control, Constructed Wetlands, Ducks, Islands,* and *Moist-Soil Management.*

Water Gardens

Small ponds usually featuring aquatic plants and perhaps colorful fish such as goldfish and koi. Water gardens are often imaginatively landscaped in a theme

Water gardens often incorporate several planting depths for submergent plants and emergents with varying stem lengths. Potted tropical plants may be moved indoors in winter.

style (Japanese garden, wildlife bog, Mediterranean) and may include a fountain or waterfall. These mini ponds are especially popular in suburban settings where space and water requirements cannot support a larger "natural" pond. Water gardens often include pumps that recirculate the water in a watertight structure consisting of a flexible plastic liner, a preformed fiberglass pool, or even a small container such as a whiskey barrel or ceramic urn. Extremely popular, water gardens are small enough to succeed as do-it-yourself projects and relatively inexpensive. Large numbers of garden supply stores and mail-order nurseries cater to the water garden trade, offering a variety of construction materials, water circulation equipment, aquatic plants, and fish. Water gardens enable homeowners (and commercial establishments) to make a dramatic landscaping statement in a small space, as well as create a psychic comfort zone promoted by the sound of splashing water. Water gardens are appreciated because they attract birds and wildlife, although there may be problems with predatory birds dining on expensive fish. Mosquitoes may lay their eggs in still water, which is why many water gardeners stock fish, which eat the larvae. Safety precautions should also be taken if small children have access to the pool. Depending on design, water filtration system, and use of fish, water gardens may require careful upkeep to prevent water-quality problems.

See *Goldfish*, *Koi*, and *Liability*.

Watershed

An area of land defined by its drainage boundaries. Watersheds are defined from the bottom up, beginning with a specific water feature (steam, river, lake, pond, or pond site) and then mapping the region of land that contributes runoff to that body of water. Large watersheds can usually be defined by reading the contours on a geological survey map and calculating acreage within those boundaries. Smaller watersheds (also called *divides*) may need to be defined by on-site

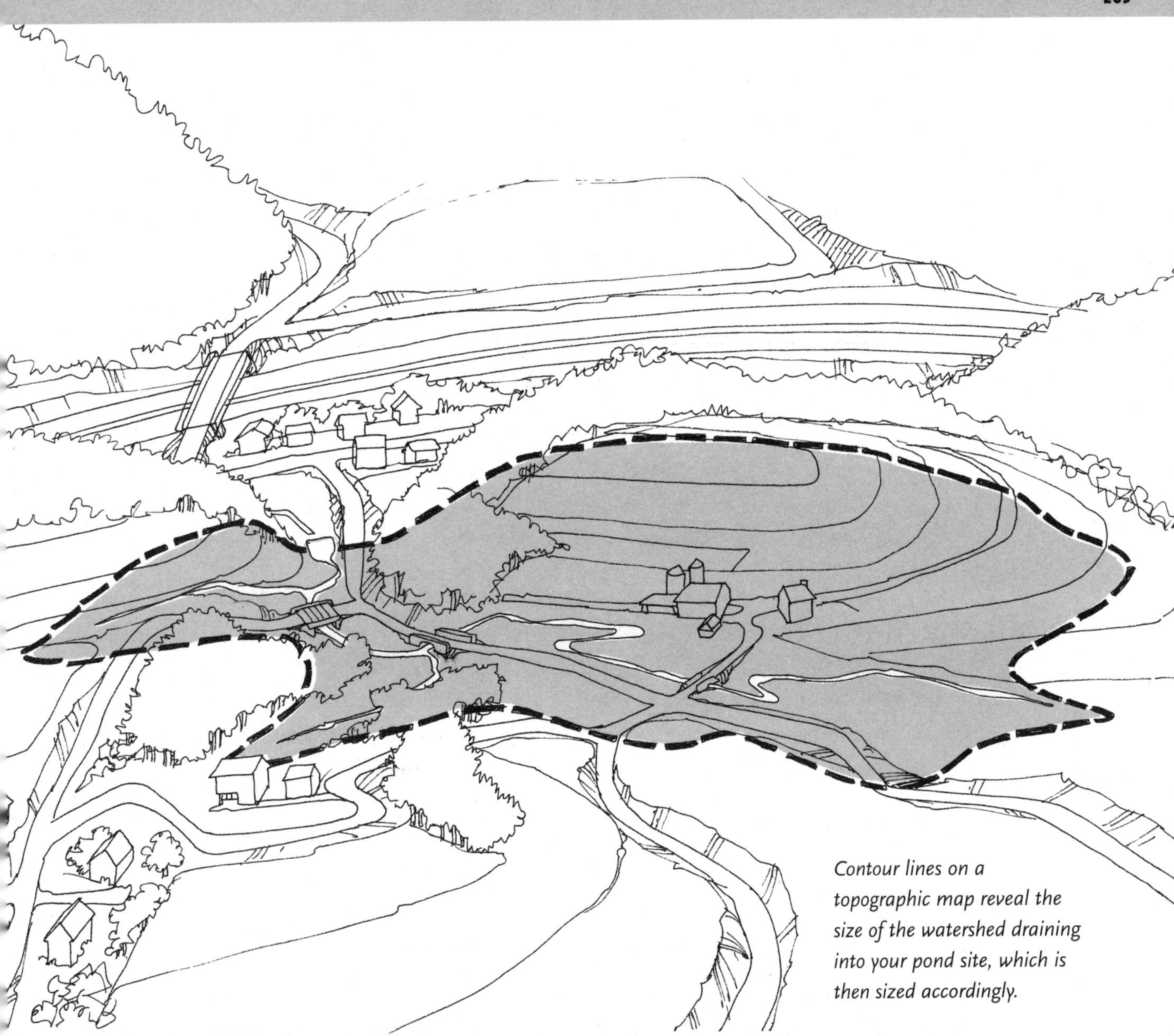

Contour lines on a topographic map reveal the size of the watershed draining into your pond site, which is then sized accordingly.

observation. The Natural Resources Conservation Service (NRCS), USDA, offers help in estimating watersheds.

Watershed evaluation is especially important where surface runoff contributes the main pond inflow. The volume of runoff water draining into a specific pond site will help determine pond size, storage capacity, and spillway requirements. Knowing the geographic characteristics of a particular watershed is important to calculating this volume. Runoff volume is affected by not only acreage size but also vegetative cover, soil type, and slope. Runoff from 10 acres of pasture will usually exceed runoff from the same amount of forested land. In general, the steeper the land, the more the runoff. Soil type will also affect watershed runoff: The higher the infiltration, the less the runoff capacity. A single watershed may contain varying terrain, which makes calculating runoff more complicated. The NRCS publishes information useful in estimating watershed runoff, including rainfall tables for different geographic regions.

Knowing the parameters of a pond watershed also enables the landowner to evaluate the potential for harmful runoff from animal waste, erosion (logging, farming, roads), septic systems, pollutants, and other bodies of water. In general, a pond watershed should be protected with erosion control practices and conservation measures to safeguard the drainage area. Land with permanent vegetation is considered best.

See *Drainage Field, Maps,* and *Natural Resources Conservation Service.*

Water Tests

Pond owners concerned about water quality may test their ponds for different elements, depending on the way the pond is used. People raising fish will be primarily concerned about dissolved oxygen levels, pH, and temperature. Recreational pond owners may want to be sure coliform bacterial levels are minimal, for swimmer safety. Those using ponds for both recreation and fish may be interested in all of these elements, and perhaps more. If the basic elements are out of balance or if the water is polluted, general pond health suffers.

Depending on the element being tested for, testing equipment ranges from simple paper strip tests to chemical kits and electronic metering. Test kits and meters can be purchased from aquacultural suppliers. The more sophisticated the test, however, the more expensive the equipment, and for some elements it may be more economical to send samples to a lab for testing.

The basic elements to test for good water quality for raising fish are dissolved oxygen, pH, alkalinity, and temperature. Good oxygen levels are required for fish health, and range between 3 and 13 milligrams per liter, depending on the species. Good pH ranges from 5 to 9 units and temperature from 45 to 90 degrees F, all figures depending on the species. Other elements considered in fish farming and general water quality may include CO_2, ammonia, nitrite, hardness, chloride, salinity, and turibidity or water transparency.

Pond owners concerned about swimmer health may want to test the water for coliform bacteria. States have differing criteria regarding fecal contamination standards for recreational water. In Vermont, public waters must test at less than 77 colonies of *E. coli* bacteria per 100 liters of water; levels in other states may vary. Other pathogens that threaten water quality include *Giardia* and *Cryptosporidium,* which are difficult and expensive to test for.

See *Ammonia, Nitrate, Nitrite, pH, Phosphorous,* and *Waterborne Illness.*

Weeds

One man's weeds may be another's prized native aquatic plants. Still, there's not usually much love lost over a pond infested with pondweeds or Eurasian water milfoil, and weed removal is the solution.

See *Biological Aquatic Plant Management, Cattails, Cleanout, Crawfish, Drawdown, Eurasian Water Milfoil, Eutrophication, Grass Carp, Invasive Exotic Plants, Maintenance, Rake, Reeds,* and *Vegetation.*

Well

Often used to supply ponds that lack sufficient groundwater or watershed runoff inflow. Well water may also be useful for raising cold-water fish because of its low temperature. There are several types of wells—artesian, static water level, and spring. Artesian wells flow under their own pressure. A true artesian well taps in to an underground aquifer at a point where stored water above the pickup point is sufficient to pressurize the water, lift it to the surface, and keep it flowing. A well drilled into an aquifer lacking such pressure will have a static water level and require a pump to deliver the water. (Artesian wells may also use a pump.) A spring well is often a cistern, tile system, or holding tank set up to store water from a flowing spring. Sometimes these springs surface at ground level; sometimes they have to be dug out by hand or backhoe, usually no deeper than 10 to 15 feet. Flow may depend on a pump or gravity.

Situations may arise where ponds need an auxiliary water supply that can't be added from natural sources such as a stream or spring, so a well is used. In the case of existing ponds that turn out not to have enough inflow, owners may be tempted to consider adding water from a household well. Unless the well has a large capacity, however, this is not generally recommended. (One contractor I talked to suggested that a household-pond well should have at least a 40-gallon-per-minute capacity.) Usually it's more practical to drill a well dedicated to pond use alone. Shallow dug wells may also be useful, although they are generally less reliable, especially during dry weather. A drilled well can be set to deliver water on a timer (for example, 15 minutes per hour), or with a water-level switch in the pond to turn off the flow at a predetermined level. This level is set just below the overflow point. It is also possible to install a cutoff switch at a minimum level in the well so the system will not be overtaxed. Delivery can be piped in below the pond water level or pumped into the air, perhaps with a spray nozzle, for aeration. Well water is often low in dissolved oxygen, and some pond owners experience oxygen problems, especially with large fish crops. Air delivery would help aerate well water.

If your existing pond turns out to have insufficient water, drilling a well is a calculated risk, and success will depend on the well's capacity in relation to pond water requirements. However, plans to build a new pond in a site lacking sufficient natural water, where a well will be needed, should probably not proceed until the well is drilled and capacity determined. Knowing well capacity will be important in determining pond size and whether membrane or clay liners may also be necessary.

See *Dowsing* and *Pumps.*

Wetlands

Wetlands are naturally saturated areas that support aquatic plants and animal life. Swamps, bogs, and marshes are examples of wetlands. Freshwater wetlands are usually fed by watershed runoff, springs, streams, or a combination of water sources. They may be flooded seasonally or year-round. Water depth is usually relatively shallow (under 6 feet), and the exchange of fresh water may be sluggish. Wetlands act as natural sponges, filtering water and retarding flooding. They support many different kinds of waterfowl and wildlife, as well as aquatic vegetation and endangered plant species. Because wetlands interfere with commercial

Wetlands prevent floods, store water during dry weather, filter pollutants, and support animal and plant life.

development and agriculture, as well as harboring disease-bearing bacteria and insects, until recently they were often drained and filled in. Awareness of the ecological benefits of wetlands has led to their protection from development.

Pond builders and owners have to be aware of the possible impact of pond construction or repair on wetland areas. Traditionally, some of the best pond-construction sites have been wetlands, which were dug out and enlarged to create a deepwater aquatic habitat suitable for recreation, raising fish, landscaping, mosquito control, and other human uses. Wetland protection laws now prevent pond construction in many wetland areas, and pond builders should check local zoning laws as well as state and federal regulations covering pond sites. Both the Natural Resources Conservation Service and the U.S. Army Corps of Engineers have maps and guidelines regulating construction in wetland areas.

As it turns out, there are practical reasons to avoid constructing a pond in a wetland area. Beavers like wetlands—they create wetlands, in fact—and ponds dug in or near wetland areas often invite beavers to take up residence. Most pond owners won't be happy with a colony of beavers taking over a pond or meddling with the spillway system. Wetlands adjacent to a new pond may introduce other unwanted aquatic life—leeches, for instance—as well as aquatic weeds, algae, and nutrients.

See *Constructed Wetlands* and *Wetland Mitigation.*

Wetland Mitigation

The U.S. Environmental Protection Agency and Army Corps of Engineers regulate construction in wetland areas under Section 404 of the Clean Water Act. Since this legislation was enacted, wetland protection has evolved from outright prohibition of wetland alteration in protected sites to various forms of "mitigation." Mitigation began as a method of wetland replacement. Developers would be allowed to destroy wetlands if they constructed equivalent wetland areas nearby. More recently, the law has been changed to allow developers to purchase credits from an approved mitigation "bank" rather than restore or create new wetlands. The theory is that preserving large wetland areas is more ecologically efficient than trying to create smaller ones artificially. Still, wetland banks themselves may be artificially constructed, and there is controversy about the effectiveness of this practice and objection from conservation groups. The mitigation concept is sometimes used by pond builders seeking permits to build in wetland areas. Landowners may offer to enhance wildlife habitats or preserve wetland areas in the pond area in order to receive a building permit.

See *Constructed Wetlands* and *Wetlands.*

Wild Japanese Millet
(Echinochloa crus-galli)

Rivaling wild rice and smartweed as a food plant used to attract waterfowl and upland birds, wild Japanese millet is often sown on mudflats or drained ponds that are later flooded during duck season. Also known as *goose grass, wild duck millet,* or *black millet.* Among shooting clubs, it's a favorite plant for attracting ducks.

See *Moist-Soil Management.*

Windpumps

For centuries windmills have been used in agriculture for water pumping and irrigation. Towering windmills with billowy cloth sails turned at the top of structures large enough for operators to live and work in. More recently we've seen compact windmills that can be assembled in a day to power water pumps used to fill ponds, or air compressors used to keep pond water oxygenated and healthy. Small wind-powered pumps are economically attractive at sites where electric pumping costs would be high or where electricity isn't available at all. Unlike electric-generating windmills, which often require consistently windy sites and batteries for power storage, air- and water-pumping systems may need less than a 5-mile-per-hour wind to operate. They're relatively inexpensive and useful at almost any pond site.

Wind-powered pumps and aerators fill ponds, transport water, and improve water quality without using electricity.

Compressed-air windpumps are especially popular with owners of agricultural ponds. Farms often include off-the-grid ponds used for livestock water or irrigation, which need to be filled or periodically replenished from another water source; windmills can do the pumping. Livestock ponds with open access to animals are liable to become polluted and structurally damaged by trampling; fencing the pond and windpumping the water to a stock tank improves water quality and has been shown to increase livestock health and weight gain. Windpump compressors also raise dissolved oxygen levels in eutrophying ponds, making the water healthy for fish.

Residential ponds benefit from wind power in many of the same ways. Problems with algae, fish-kills, and siltation can be solved by aeration. Pumping compressed air during winter can keep a pond ice-free for improved waterfowl and fish habitat. Aeration removes sulfur and iron from tainted water, making it potable for household use. Aerating windmills are also being used to help clean up groundwater contaminated by leaks from gas storage tanks.

See *Aeration.*

Zooplankton

Microscopic multicellular aquatic creatures that live in salt water, rivers, lakes, and ponds. They thrive in slow-moving freshwater environments such as ponds, grazing on algae and providing food for fish and amphibians higher up the food chain. Crustaceans and rotifers make up the majority of zooplankton, and biologists are still discovering new species. A healthy, well-balanced zooplankton population is essential to good pond water quality. Scientists have seen evidence that pollution and introduction of non-native species can adversely affect zooplankton, which in turn degrades water quality, particularly through increases in algal blooms. Pond owners should be aware that chemicals, dyes, and certain predatory fish can crash the beneficial zooplankton population, setting the stage for algal problems.

Fish are one of the major controlling factors of zooplankton. Smaller species of fish will be the strongest predators on big zooplankton, which are the best alga grazers. Too many smaller fish (stunted bluegills, for example) can result in a population of predominantly small, inefficient zooplankton grazers, often leading to greening of the pond. Adding larger fish, such as bass, can help reestablish the beneficial larger zooplankton and improve water quality. A favorable nitrogen-to-phosphorous ratio is also important to a healthy zooplankton population, as well as good water quality. Transfers of pond water for irrigation and other uses, and replacement from streams, can also adversely affect zooplankton.

See *Alga* and *Biological Aquatic Plant Management.*

Appendix A: Conversion Formulas

1 acre = 43,560 square feet

Surface acre of pond = $\frac{\text{length x width}}{43{,}560}$

Acre feet = $\frac{\text{length x width x average depth}}{43{,}560}$

1 pound = 16 oz. = 454 grams

1 ounce = 28.35 grams

1 kilogram = 2.2 pounds

1 cubic foot = 62.4 pounds
= 7.5 gallons of water

1 acre-foot of water = 2,718,000 pounds
= 326,000 gallons
= 3,800 grams
= 3,785 liters

1 liter of water = 0.264 gallons

1 part per million (ppm) requires:

2.7 pounds per acre-foot
0.0038 grams per gallon
0.0283 grams per cubic foot

LIQUID

1 gallon	= 4 quarts
	= 8 pints
1 pint	= 16 ounces
1 cup	= 8 ounces
1 tablespoon	= 1/2 ounce

AREA

1 acre	= a square with 209 feet per side
1 acre	= a circle with a diameter of 235 feet

Appendix B: Formulas for Determining the Surface Acreage of a Pond

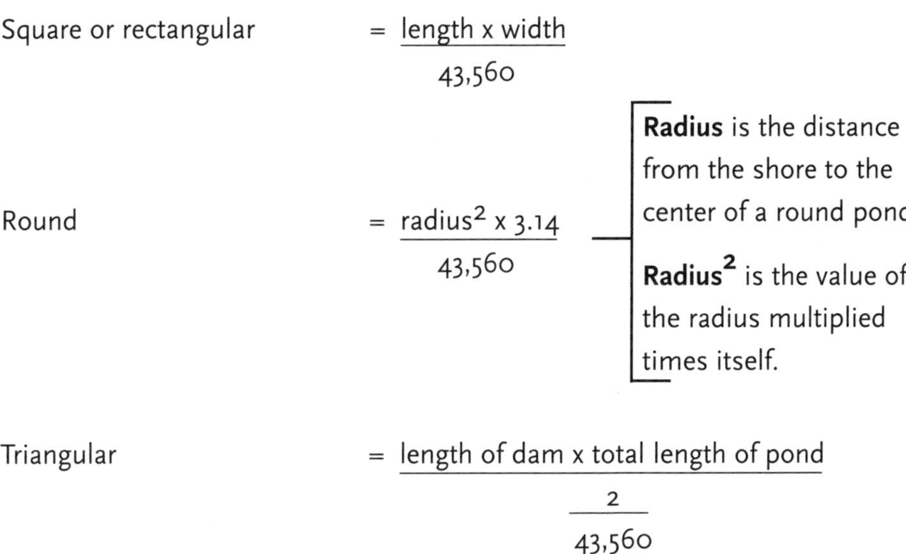

Square or rectangular $= \dfrac{\text{length x width}}{43{,}560}$

Round $= \dfrac{\text{radius}^2 \text{ x } 3.14}{43{,}560}$

Radius is the distance from the shore to the center of a round pond.

Radius^2 is the value of the radius multiplied times itself.

Triangular $= \dfrac{\dfrac{\text{length of dam x total length of pond}}{2}}{43{,}560}$

Average depth is determined by making seven transects per 2 acres of water, recording depths at three-foot intervals along each transect, and averaging these figures.

Bibliography

BOOKS

ACKEFORS, HUNER, AND KONIKOFF. *Introduction to the General Principles of Aquaculture.* Food Products Press, 1994.

BARDACH, RYTHER, AND MCLARNEY. *Aquaculture.* Wiley-Interscience, 1972.

BENNETT, GEORGE W. *Management of Lakes and Ponds.* Van Nostrand Reinhold, 1970.

BIRD, CHRISTOPHER. *The Divining Hand.* Whitford Press, 1993.

BRING AND WAYEMBERGH. *Japanese Gardens.* McGraw-Hill, 1981.

BURNS, MAX. *Cottage Water Systems.* Cottage Life Publishing, 1993.

CADUTO, MICHAEL J. *Pond and Brook.* University Press of New England, 1985, 1990.

CAMPBELL, STU. *The Home Water Supply.* Garden Way Publishing, 1983.

COOKE, WELCH, PETERSON, NEWROTH. *Restoration and Management of Lakes and Reservoirs.* Lewis Publishers, 1993.

GILMER, MAUREEN. *Living on Flood Plains and Wetlands.* Taylor Publishing Company, 1995.

GLATTSTEIN, JUDY. *Waterscaping.* Garden Way Publishing, 1994.

GREENOAK, FRANCESCA. *Water Features for Small Gardens.* Trafalgar Square Publishing, 1996.

HAMMER, DONALD A. *Creating Freshwater Wetlands.* Lewis Publishers, 1992.

HENDERSON, CARROL L. *Landscaping for Wildlife.* Minnesota Department of Natural Resources, 1987.

How to Identify and Control Water Weeds and Algae. Applied Biochemists, 1976.

HUNER, JAY V. *Eighteen Years of Jay V. Huner* & Farm Pond Harvest *Magazine.* Professional Sportsmans Publishing, 1994.

KLOTS, ELSIE B. *The New Field Book of Freshwater Life.* G. P. Putnam's Sons, 1966.

Management of Small Lakes and Ponds in Illinois. Illinois Department of Conservation, 1986.

MCCLANE, A. J. *McClane's Field Guide to Freshwater Fishes of North America.* Henry Holt and Company, 1978.

MCCOMAS, STEVE. *Lake Smarts.* Terrene Institute, 1993.

MCRAVEN, CHARLES. *Stonework.* Storey Publishing, 1997.

NASH, HELEN. *The Pond Doctor.* Sterling Publishing Company, 1994.

NASH, HELEN, AND MARILYN M. COOK. *Water Gardening Basics.* Sterling Publishing Company, 1999.

NIERING, WILLIAM A. *Wetlands.* Alfred A. Knopf, 1985.

PRATHER, KERRY W. *A Guide to the Management of Farm Ponds in Kentucky.* Kentucky Department of Fish and Wildlife Resources.

REED, CRITES, MIDDLEBROOKS. *Natural Systems for Waste Management and Treatment.* McGraw-Hill, 1995.

SCHAEFFER, JOHN, AND THE REAL GOOD STAFF. *Solar Living Sourcebook.* Chelsea Green Publishing, 1996.

STERN, CAROLYN. *Ponds: Building, Maintaining, Enjoying.* Progressive Farmer, 1996.

THOMAS, CHARLES B. *Water Gardens.* Houghton Mifflin, 1997.

THOMAS, CHARLES B. AND RICHARD M. COOGLE. *Ortho's All About Building Waterfalls, Pools, and Streams.* Meredith Books, 2002.

THUNHORST, GWENDOLYN A. *Wetland Planting Guide for the Northeastern United States.* Environmental Concern, 1993.

WARREN, SUSAN. *Lake and Pond Plants.* Vermont Department of Environmental Conservation, 1990.

WHITNER, JAN. *Stonescaping.* Garden Way Publishing, 1992.

PERIODICALS

Aquaculture Magazine
16 Church Street
Asheville, NC 28801

Farm Pond Harvest Magazine
1390 North 14500 E Road
Momence, IL 60954

Fish Farming News
P.O. Box 37
Stonington, ME 04681

Land and Water
P.O. Box 1197
Fort Dodge, IA 50501

Pond Boss
P.O. Box 12
Sadler, TX 76264

Pondkeeper Magazine
100 Whitetail Court
Duncansville, PA 16635

Water Gardening Magazine
P.O. Box 607
St. John, IN 46373

CATALOGS

Agri Drain Corporation
P.O. Box 458
Adair, IA 50002
641-742-5211

Aquatic Eco-Systems
1767 Benbow Court
Apopka, FL 32703
407-886-3939

Lilypons Water Gardens
6800 Lilypons Road
P.O. Box 10
Buckeystown, MD 21717-0010
1-800-999-5459

Malibu Water Resources
P.O. Box 55155
Beverly Hills, CA 90210
1-800-470-4602

Stoney Creek Equipment Co.
11073 Peach Avenue
Grant, MI 49327
1-800-448-3873

The Earth Ponds Library

"Tim Matson is the guru of ponds." —*Albany Times-Union*

Earth Ponds

The Country Pond Maker's Guide to Building, Maintenance and Restoration

Tim Matson's classic guide, first published in 1982, remains the standard reference for pond owners and builders. Here is everything you need to know to plan, dig, sculpt, maintain, and enjoy your pond, and how to keep it healthy for years.

$19.95 (Can. $28.99), ISBN 0-88150-155-7, paperback, 152 pages

Earth Ponds Sourcebook

The Pond Owner's Manual and Resource Guide
New Revised Edition!

The *Earth Ponds Sourcebook* presents hundreds of additional tips, techniques, and resources, including how to plan a pond to attract wildlife; where to buy equipment and materials; how to build rafts, docks, and gazebos; and how to deal with common problems like weeds, algae, and crayfish.

$21.95 (Can. $33.00), ISBN 0-88150-612-5, paperback, 182 pages

The Countryman Press
Woodstock, Vermont

We offer many more books on gardening, country living, food and cooking, nature, and other subjects. Our books are available at bookstores everywhere. For more information or a free catalog, please call 1-800-245-4151, or write to us at The Countryman Press, P.O. Box 748, Woodstock, Vermont 05091. You can find us on the Internet at www.countrymanpress.com